혼공

기초영문법

혼공 허준석 지음

L2

혼공 기초 영문법 Level 2

1판 1쇄 2022년 2월 7일
1판 6쇄 2025년 2월 10일

지은이 허준석
표지디자인 박새롬
내지디자인 황지영
표지그림 김효지
마케팅 두잉글 사업본부
브랜드 혼공북스
펴낸곳 (주)혼공유니버스
출판등록 제2021-000288호
주 소 04033 서울특별시 마포구 양화로 113 4층(서교동)
전자메일 team@hongong.co.kr

ISBN 979-11-976810-4-2 13740

혼공!

영어 공부 참 어렵습니다. 특히, 영문법이란 말을 들으면 어디서부터 시작해야 할지 앞이 깜깜합니다. 저 역시도 그러한 경험을 했었기에, 세상에서 가장 쉽게 영문법 공부를 할 수 있는 책이나 강의가 있으면 좋겠다고 생각을 했습니다. 그래서, 혼공 기초 영문법이 탄생했습니다. 짧은 이론, 반복되는 개념, 쓰기 위주의 연습을 통해 그 동안 공부해오던 방식을 벗어날 수 있을 것입니다.

영문법에는 규칙도 많고, 예외도 참 많습니다. 많은 사람들은 예외를 보면서 겁에 질려 영어 공부를 중단하게 됩니다. 그럴 필요 없습니다. 왜 규칙이 생겼는지 이해하고, 조금 외우고, 예외는 이런 게 있구나 하고 넘어가도 됩니다. 이렇게 반복해서 학습하다보면 애쓰지 않아도 예외까지 완벽하게 익혀지게 됩니다. 반대로, 처음부터 예외를 파고들어 공부한다면, 실수할까봐 영어로 말하기도 쓰기도 제대로 못하게 됩니다.

혼공 영어는 결국 말하고, 실전에서 쓸 수 있는 영어를 목표로 하고 있습니다. 쉽게 공부해서 자신감을 찾고, 점점 더 깊이 있는 공부를 하면서 내가 원하는 영어 실력에 도달하길 바랍니다. 재미있게 끝까지 간다면 무조건 성공합니다. 끈기를 가지고 혼공하세요!

혼공 허준석 드림

오리엔테이션

 혼공개념 | 단어암기법

1 짧게 자주 봐라.

2 무조건 베껴 쓰지 마라.

3 반드시 발음해봐야 한다.

4 예문으로 마무리 해야 한다.

 혼공개념 | 발음 기호 읽기

모르는 단어의 발음 기호를 찾아서 읽어 보자. 동시에, 반드시 원어민 발음을 듣고 따라하는 습관을 처음부터 길러야 한다.

1 모음 소리 내기

[a]	[e] [ɛ]	[æ]	[i] [ɪ]	[ɔ]
아	에	애 (입 크게 벌리고)	이	오 ('오'와 '아'의 중간)

[u] [ʊ]	[ə]	[ʌ]	[:]	[ˈ][ˌ]
우	어	어	장음 길게 발음	제 1, 2강세 힘줘서 발음

2 모음 + 모음 소리 내기

[ai]	[ei]	[au]	[ɔi]	[ou]	[iə]	[ɛə]	[uə]

3 쉬운 자음

[b]	[p]	[d]	[t]	[f]	[v]
book	peace	dog	toy	face	victory
브	프	드	트	프	브
					윗니를 아랫입술에 대고 발음

[θ]	[ð]	[m]	[n]	[ŋ]	[h]
think	this	moon	name	song	house
뜨	드	므	느	응	흐
윗니와 아랫니 사이에 혀를 살짝 물고 발음				받침처럼 쓰임	

4 낯선 자음

[g]	[k]	[s]	[z]	[ʃ]	[ʒ]
green	king	sea	zoo	ship	television
그	크	스	즈	쉬	지

[l]	[r]	[tʃ]	[dʒ]	[w]	[j]
love	rose	cheese	jacket	world	yellow
르	(으)르	취	쥐	우	여
	혀를 말고 발음				뒷발음과 섞임

contents

contents

혼공 기초 영문법
LEVEL 2

혼공 기초 영문법
LEVEL 2

1형식 문장

> 🔵 **혼공개념** 1형식 문장이란?

1 ~은, 는, 이, 가 + ~한다

　예 A leaf fell.

2 ~은, 는, 이, 가 + ~한다 + ~에서(장소)

　예 A leaf fell on the ground.

3 ~은, 는, 이, 가 + ~한다 + ~에(시간)

　예 A leaf fell in the morning.

4 ~은, 는, 이, 가 + ~한다 + ~에서(장소) + ~에(시간)

　예 A leaf fell on the ground in the morning.

5 ~은, 는, 이, 가 + ~한다 + ~하게(부사)

　예 A leaf fell slowly.

혼공 팁

같은 동사라도 문장의 구조에 따라 의미가 달라진다.

　예 This car sells well.(팔린다), He sold the car in the morning.(팔았다)

> 🔵 **혼공개념** There is / are

1 의미: ~가 있다(발견)

There is + 단수명사	There are + 복수명사
There is an apple.	There are two apples.

혼공 연습

 아래 <보기> 속의 예시처럼 주어진 문장을 분석하시오.

<보기> ~은, 는, 이, 가 + ~한다

~은, 는, 이, 가 + ~한다 + ~에서(장소)

~은, 는, 이, 가 + ~한다 + ~에(시간)

~은, 는, 이, 가 + ~한다 + ~에서(장소) + ~에(시간)

~은, 는, 이, 가 + ~한다 + ~하게(부사)

예 A leaf / fell / in the morning.
　　~이　　~한다　　~에(시간)

① We / live / in Korea.

_____

② The door / opened / slowly.

_____

③ Linda / jogs / in the morning.

_____

④ A leaf / fell / on the ground / in the morning.

_____

⑤ The flower / died / last night.

_____

A 다음 문장을 / 으로 끊고 우리말 해석을 쓰시오.

① Jason lives in Russia.

_____

② The patient died suddenly.

_____

③ They work on Saturdays.

_____

④ A lot of students stood in the playground.

_____

β 우리말 의미와 같도록 주어진 표현을 올바르게 배열하시오.

① 해는 동쪽에서 뜬다.　　　in the east / the sun / rises

_____

② 그들은 매일 학교에 간다.　　to school / they / every day / go

_____

③ 그 택시는 호텔에 도착했다.　at / the taxi / the hotel / arrived

_____

④ 그의 주위에 많은 팬들이 있었다. were / a lot of / fans / around / him / there

_____

A. 다음 문장을 ①번의 예시처럼 / 긋고, 우리말 해석을 쓰시오.

① We / live / in Korea.

　　우리는　/　산다　/　한국에(서)

② The door opened slowly.

_____

③ Linda jogs in the morning.

_____

④ A leaf fell on the ground in the morning.

_____

⑤ The flower died last night.

_____

⑥ The sun rises in the east.

_____

⑦ They go to school every day.

_____

⑧ The taxi arrived at the hotel.

_____

⑨ There were a lot of fans around him.

_____

정답 ② The door / opened / slowly. 그 문은 / 열렸다 / 천천히 ③ Linda / jogs / in the morning. Linda는 / 조깅한다 / 아침에 ④ A leaf / fell / on the ground / in the morning. 나뭇잎 하나가 / 떨어졌다 / 땅바닥으로 / 아침에 ⑤ The flower / died / last night. 그 꽃은 / 죽었다 / 어젯밤에 ⑥ The sun / rises / in the east. 해는 / 뜬다 / 동쪽에서 ⑦ They / go / to school / every day. 그들은 / 간다 / 학교에 / 매일 ⑧ The taxi / arrived / at the hotel. 그 택시는 / 도착했다 / 호텔에 ⑨ There were / a lot of fans / around him. 있었다 / 많은 팬들이 / 그의 주위에

2형식 문장

1 ~은, 는, 이, 가 + ~이다/되다 + 직업, 직책, 신분...

　예 He <u>is</u> a scientist. 　　　　　She <u>is</u> an actress.

　　He <u>became</u> a teacher.

2 ~은, 는, 이, 가 + ~이다 + 상태

　예 He <u>is</u> always happy.

　　You <u>must be</u> hungry.

3 ~은, 는, 이, 가 + ~되다 + 상태

　예 He <u>became</u> unhappy. 　　　The eggs <u>went</u> bad.

　　The leaves <u>turned</u> brown. 　　She <u>got</u> mad.

혼공 팁

　go, turn, run, grow, fall, come, get...은 2형식에서 '~가 되다'라는 의미로 해석하면 자연스럽다.

　예 Her dream came true. 　　The baby fell asleep.

4 ~은, 는, 이, 가 + 감각동사 + 상태

　예 The steak <u>smells</u> good. It <u>tastes</u> sour.

혼공 팁

　감각동사에는 feel, smell, sound, taste... 등이 있다.

　예 My hands <u>feel</u> cold.

혼공 연습

 아래 <보기> 속의 예시처럼 주어진 문장을 분석하시오.

<보기>   ~은, 는, 이, 가 + ~이다/되다 + 직업, 직책, 신분…

　　　　~은, 는, 이, 가 + ~이다 + 상태

　　　　~은, 는, 이, 가 + ~되다 + 상태

　　　　~은, 는, 이, 가 + 감각동사 + 상태

　　　　예 He / is / a scientist.

　　　　　~는 ~이다   직업, 직책, 신분…

① He / became / a teacher.

_____

② You / must be / hungry.

_____

③ The leaves / turned / brown.

_____

④ The baby / fell / asleep.

_____

⑤ The steak / smells / good.

_____

A 다음 문장을 / 으로 끊고 우리말 해석을 쓰시오.

① The soup tastes salty.

_____

② My cousin is an English teacher.

_____

③ The music sounds beautiful.

_____

④ Your dad looks really upset.

_____

B 다음 우리말 의미를 참고하여 빈칸을 채우시오.

① 그 소년은 미래에 의사가 될 것이다

The boy _____ _____ a _____ in the future.

② 레몬은 신맛이 난다.

Lemons _____ sour.

③ 그 작은 소녀는 아주 피곤해 보였다.

The little _____ _____ very _____.

④ 나는 아주 배가 고팠었다.

I _____ very _____.

A. 다음 문장을 1번의 예시처럼 / 긋고, 우리말 해석을 쓰시오.

① He / became / a teacher.

그는 / 되었다 / 선생님

② The leaves turned brown.

_____

③ The baby fell asleep.

_____

④ My cousin is an English teacher.

_____

⑤ The music sounds beautiful.

_____

⑥ Your dad looks really upset.

_____

⑦ Lemons taste sour.

_____

⑧ The little girl looked very tired.

_____

정답 ② The leaves / turned / brown. 잎들은 / 되었다 / 갈색 ③ The baby / fell / asleep. 그 아기는 / 되었다 / 잠든 ④ My cousin / is / an English teacher. 내 사촌은 / 이다 / 영어 선생님 ⑤ The music / sounds / beautiful. 그 음악은 / 들린다 / 아름다운 ⑥ Your dad / looks / really upset. 너의 아빠는 / 보인다 / 정말 화난 ⑦ Lemons / taste / sour. 레몬은 / 맛이 난다 / 신 ⑧ The little girl / looked / very tired. 그 작은 소녀는 / 보였다 / 아주 피곤한

3형식 문장

🔆 **혼공개념** 3형식 문장이란?

1 ~은, 는, 이, 가 + ~한다 + (사람, 사물)을, 를

예 I watched a movie.　　We saw him.

Harry cleaned his house.

2 ~은, 는, 이, 가 + ~한다 + (사람, 사물)을, 를 + 시간(장소)

예 I watched a movie in the theater.

We saw him in the park.

Harry cleaned his house on Sunday.

Do not put all your eggs in one basket.

3 ~은, 는, 이, 가 + ~한다 + (사람, 사물)을, 를 + 기타

예 Jane sold the computer to me.

Jane sold the computer to me last year.

혼공 팁

3형식 문장에서 '을, 를' 대신 '~에'라고 해석할 때 더 자연스러운 경우도 있다.

예 Someone entered the room.

　　　　　　　　　　　그 방에

아래 <보기> 속의 예시처럼 주어진 문장을 분석하시오.

<보기> ~은, 는, 이, 가 + ~한다 + (사람, 사물)을, 를

~은, 는, 이, 가 + ~한다 + (사람, 사물)을, 를 + 시간(장소)

~은, 는, 이, 가 + ~한다 + (사람, 사물)을, 를 + 기타

예 I / watched / a movie.

~는   ~한다   ~를

① Harry / cleaned / his house.

_____

② I / watched / a movie / in the theater.

_____

③ We / saw / him / in the park.

_____

④ Do not put / all your eggs / in one basket.

_____

⑤ Jane / sold / the computer / to me / last year.

_____

A 다음 문장을 / 으로 끊고 우리말 해석을 쓰시오.

① Fine clothes make the man.

_____

② My grandma heated the water in the pot.

_____

③ He took a bus to Seoul last night.

_____

④ Kevin blamed me for the mistake.

_____

B 다음 우리말 의미를 참고하여 빈칸을 채우시오.

① 그녀는 밤에 책들을 읽는다.

She _____ _____ at _____.

② 나는 찌개에 소금을 약간 넣었다.

I _____ some _____ in the soup.

③ 우리 엄마는 작년에 새 가방을 사지 않으셨다.

My mom didn't _____ a new _____ _____ year.

④ 나는 이 시계에 100달러를 지불했다.

I _____ $100 for _____ _____.

A. 다음 문장을 1번의 예시처럼 / 긋고, 우리말 해석을 쓰시오.

① Harry / cleaned / his house.
　　Harry는 / 청소했다 / 그의 방을

② I watched a movie in the theater.

_____

③ Jane sold the computer to me last year.

_____

④ My grandma heated the water in the pot.

_____

⑤ He took a bus to Seoul last night.

_____

⑥ Kevin blamed me for the mistake.

_____

⑦ I put some salt in the soup.

_____

⑧ I paid $100 for this watch.

_____

정답 ② I / watched / a movie / in the theater. 나는 / 보았다 / 영화 한 편을 / 그 극장에서　③ Jane / sold / the computer / to me / last year. Jane은 / 팔았다 / 그 컴퓨터를 / 나에게 / 작년에　④ My grandma / heated / the water / in the pot. 내 할머니는 / 데웠다 / 물을 / 냄비에 있는　⑤ He / took / a bus / to Seoul / last night. 그는 / 탔다 / 버스를 / 서울로 가는 / 어젯밤에　⑥ Kevin / blamed / me / for the mistake. Kevin은 / 비난했다 / 나를 / 그 실수로　⑦ I / put / some salt / in the soup. 나는 / 넣었다 / 약간의 소금을 / 그 찌개에　⑧ I / paid / $100 / for this watch. 나는 / 지불했다 / 100달러를 / 이 시계를 위해

4형식 문장

🔆 **혼공개념** | 4형식 문장이란?

1 ~은, 는, 이, 가 + 준다 + ~(사람)에게 + ~(사물)을

> 예 My dad <u>gave</u> me a book.   She <u>sent</u> me a letter.
>
> He <u>bought</u> me a ring.   Tom <u>made</u> me a toy.
>
> Kevin <u>asked</u> me a question.

혼공 팁

같은 동사라도 문장의 형식(구조)에 따라 해석을 달리 해야 한다. 4형식에 쓰인 동사들은
대부분 '~주다'라고 해석하면 자연스럽다.

> 예 My mom didn't <u>buy</u> a new bag last year. (사다)
>
> He <u>bought</u> me a ring. (사주다)

🔆 **혼공개념** | 4형식 문장의 3형식 문장으로 전환

 사람과 사물의 위치를 바꿈

1) 진지사 to를 쓰는 경우: give, tell, lend, show, send, bring, teach...

> 예 My dad gave <u>me a book</u>. (4형식) ⇒ My dad gave <u>a book to me</u>. (3형식)

2) 전치사 for를 쓰는 경우: buy, make, get, find...

> 예 He bought <u>me a book</u>. (4형식) ⇒ He bought <u>a book for me</u>. (3형식)

3) 전치사 of를 쓰는 경우: ask

> 예 Kevin asked <u>me a question</u>. (4형식) ⇒ Kevin asked <u>a question of me</u>. (3형식)

아래 <보기>를 참고하여 주어진 문장을 해석하시오.

> <보기> ~은, 는, 이, 가 + 준다 + ~(사람)에게 + ~(사물)을
>
> 예 My dad / gave / me / a book.
>   내 아빠는   주었다   나에게   책을

① She / sent / me / a letter.

_____

② He / bought / me / a ring.

_____

③ Tom / made / me / a toy.

_____

④ Kevin / asked / me / a question.

_____

⑤ You / can buy / her / a new car.

_____

⑥ She / has to send / him / an email.

_____

A 다음 문장을 / 으로 끊고 우리말 해석을 쓰시오.

① My father gives me a lot of advice.

_____

② I will tell you a funny story.

_____

③ She bought me a bicycle for my birthday.

_____

④ My mom made him an apple pie.

_____

B 빈칸을 채워 같은 의미를 가진 문장을 완성하시오.

① I'll make you a kite.

= I'll make _____.

② Mr. Kim teaches me English this year.

= Mr. Kim teaches _____.

③ The thief didn't tell us the truth.

= The thief didn't _____.

④ She asked me a lot of questions.

= _____.

혼공
복습

A. 다음 문장을 1번의 예시처럼 / 긋고, 우리말 해석을 쓰시오.

① He / bought / me / a ring.
　　그는 / 사줬다 / 나에게 / 반지를

② Tom made me a toy.
　　_____

③ Kevin asked me a question.
　　_____

④ She has to send him an email.
　　_____

⑤ My father gives me a lot of advice.
　　_____

⑥ She bought me a bicycle for my birthday.
　　_____

⑦ Mr. Kim teaches me English this year.
　　_____

⑧ The thief didn't tell us the truth.
　　_____

5형식 문장

혼공개념 5형식 문장이란?

1 ~은, 는, 이, 가 + ~한다 + (사람, 사물)을 + 이름, 직업

[예] My mom <u>made</u> me a famous tennis player.

We <u>call</u> him Jack.   My grandpa <u>named</u> me Jun.

2 ~은, 는, 이, 가 + ~한다 + (사람, 사물)을 + 상태

[예] They <u>painted</u> the walls blue.

My success <u>made</u> them happy.

I <u>thought</u> him handsome.

This jacket <u>will keep</u> you warm.

She <u>found</u> the movie boring.

3 ~은, 는, 이, 가 + ~한다 + (사람, 사물)은, 는, 이, 가 + 동작

[예] I <u>want</u> you to eat more.

Ms. Park <u>helped</u> us clean the car.

He will <u>get</u> the man to fix his car.

혼공 팁

같은 동사라도 문장의 형식(구조)에 따라 해석을 달리 해야 한다. make와 같은 동사는 형식에 따라 다양한 의미로 쓰인다.

[예] She <u>made</u> coffee for me. (3형식)

She <u>made</u> me an apple pie. (4형식)

She <u>made</u> Chloe read the book. (5형식)

혼공 연습

 아래 <보기> 속의 예시를 참고하여 주어진 문장을 해석하시오.

<보기> ~은, 는, 이, 가 + ~한다 + (사람, 사물)을 + 이름, 직업

~은, 는, 이, 가 + ~한다 + (사람, 사물)을 + 상태

~은, 는, 이, 가 + ~한다 + (사람, 사물)은, 는, 이, 가 + 동작

예 We / call / him / Jack.

우리는 부른다   그를   Jack이라고

① My mom / made / me / a famous tennis player.

_____

② My grandpa / named / me / Jun.

_____

③ They / painted / the walls / blue.

_____

④ This jacket / will keep / you / warm.

_____

⑤ Ms. Park / helped / us / clean the car.

_____

⑥ She / made / Chloe / read the book.

_____

A 다음 문장을 / 으로 끊고 우리말 해석을 쓰시오.

① Jun always makes us laugh.

_____

② Jogging can keep you healthy.

_____

③ We called him Jack.

_____

④ My parents didn't allow me to go out.

_____

B 다음 우리말 의미를 참고하여 빈칸을 채우시오.

① 나는 내 집을 하얀색으로 칠할 것이다.

I will _____.

② 이 선생님은 내가 그 수학 문제를 푸는 것을 도와주셨다.

Mr. Yi _____ the math problem.

③ 너는 너의 몸을 튼튼하게 유지해야 한다. (keep)

You must _____.

④ 우리는 Cindy를 팀의 주장으로 선출했다. (elect)

_____ captain of the team.

A. 다음 문장을 1번의 예시처럼 / 긋고, 우리말 해석을 쓰시오.

① My mom / made / me / a famous tennis player.
내 엄마는 / 만들었다 / 나를/ 유명한 테니스 선수로

② They painted the walls blue.

_____

③ Ms. Park helped us clean the car.

_____

④ She made Chloe read the book.

_____

⑤ Jogging can keep you healthy.

_____

⑥ My parents didn't allow me to go out.

_____

⑦ You must keep your body strong.

_____

⑧ We elected Cindy captain of the team.

_____

정답 ② They / painted / the walls / blue. 그들은 / 페인트칠했다 / 그 벽들을 / 파란색으로 ③ Ms. Park / helped / us / clean the car. 박 선생님은 / 도왔다 / 우리들이 / 그 차를 청소하도록 ④ She / made / Chloe / read the book. 그녀는 / 만들었다 / Chloe가 / 그 책을 읽도록 ⑤ Jogging / can keep / you / healthy. 조깅은 / 유지시킬 수 있다 / 너를 / 건강한 ⑥ My parents / didn't allow / me / to go out. 내 부모님들은 / 허락하지 않았다 / 내가 / 나가도록 ⑦ You / must keep / your body / strong. 너는 / 반드시 유지해야 한다 / 너의 몸을 / 강한 ⑧ We / elected / Cindy / captain of the team. 우리는 / 선출했다 / Cindy를 / 팀의 주장으로

재귀대명사

재귀대명사란?

1 ~self, ~selves 가 붙는 대명사: '~자신, ~스스로'를 의미함

예 I did it myself! Jun loves himself.

I	you	he/she/it
myself	yourself	himself / herself / itself
we	you	they
ourselves	yourselves	themselves

재귀대명사의 용법

1 재귀 용법: 문장에서 필요한 부분으로 쓰임

예 He killed himself.　　Amanda loves herself.

예 She loves her. (She≠her)

2 강조 용법: 강조하고 싶은 말 뒤나 문장 뒤에 놓여서 쓰임

예 I myself did it! We did our homework ourselves.

혼공 팁

재귀대명사를 생략하여 말이 되면 '강조 용법', 그렇지 않으면 '재귀 용법'이다.

재귀대명사의 관용적 표현

by oneself 혼자서	for oneself 스스로, 혼자 힘으로
of itself 저절로	enjoy oneself 즐기다
help oneself to ~을 맘껏 즐기다	behave oneself 예의바르게 행하다
make oneself at home (집처럼) 편하게 하다	

A 다음 단어와 관계된 재귀대명사를 쓰시오.

① I _____ she _____

② he _____ it _____

③ you _____ _____

④ we _____ they _____

β 빈칸에 적절한 재귀대명사를 쓰시오.

① I did it _____!

② Amanda loves _____.

③ He killed _____.

④ We did our homework _____.

C 밑줄 친 재귀대명사의 관용적 표현에 주의하여 우리말로 해석하시오.

① She did it <u>by herself</u>.

_____

② We <u>enjoyed ourselves</u> at the party.

_____

③ You should <u>behave yourself</u>.

_____

A 다음 밑줄 친 단어를 재귀대명사로 고치고 생략할 수 있는지 O, X 중 하나를 선택하시오.

① I cut <u>me</u>.

_____ 생략 (O, X)

② Susan sometimes talks to <u>her</u>.

_____ 생략 (O, X)

③ He didn't like the actress, but he liked the movie <u>it</u>.

_____ 생략 (O, X)

④ The students can do everything by <u>them</u>.

_____ 생략 (O, X)

⑤ My father made the treehouse <u>him</u>.

_____ 생략 (O, X)

B 다음 우리말 의미를 참고하여 빈칸을 채우시오.

① 샐러드 마음껏 드세요.

Please _____ _____ to the salad.

② Chloe는 그녀 자신을 문 뒤에 숨겼다(숨었다).

Chloe hid _____ behind the _____.

③ 그녀는 8살이지만, 스스로 요리할 수 있다.

She is 8 years _____, but she can _____ for _____.

A. 다음 빈칸을 예시처럼 채우시오.

I	you	he/she/it
myself		
we	you	they

by oneself	혼자서	for oneself	
of itself		enjoy oneself	
help oneself to		behave oneself	
make oneself at home			

B. 다음 문장을 우리말로 해석하시오.

① You should behave yourself.

_____

② We enjoyed ourselves at the party.

_____

③ Susan sometimes talks to herself.

_____

④ He didn't like the actress, but he liked the movie itself.

_____

⑤ Chloe hid herself behind the door.

_____

정답 A의 정답은 앞 페이지의 오늘 공부했던 박스를 참고하세요. ① 너는 행동을 바르게 해야 한다. ② 우리는 파티에서 즐거운 시간을 보냈다. ③ Susan은 때때로 자기 자신에게 말한다(혼잣말 한다). ④ 그는 그 여배우가 마음에 들지 않았지만, 영화 그 자체는 좋아했다. ⑤ Chloe는 문 뒤에 자신을 숨겼다(숨었다).

부정대명사

1 막연한 사람이나 사물의 수량을 나타낼 때 쓰는 대명사

some / any	all		both
약간의 / 약간의, 어떤 ~도	모든		둘 다
neither	none	every	each
둘 다 ~가 아닌	아무도 ~아닌(둘 이상)	모든	각각의, 개개의

예 Do you have <u>any</u> questions?   Yes, I have <u>some</u> questions.

I love <u>all</u> of them.   I love <u>both</u> of them.

I like <u>neither</u> of them.   <u>Every</u> day seemed the same.

<u>Each</u> of the students has his or her own locker.

<u>None</u> of the boys went hiking last weekend.

혼공개념   one, the other, another, some, others, the others의 쓰임

혼공 연습

A 다음 우리말과 일치하는 부정대명사를 쓰시오.

① 모든 a_____ 둘 다 _____

② 약간의 _____ 모든 e_____

③ 각각의 _____ 둘 다 _____

④ 둘 다 ~가 아닌 _____ 모든 e_____

⑤ 어떤 ~도 _____ 아무도 ~아닌 _____

B 빈칸에 적절한 부정대명사를 쓰시오.

① 질문 좀 있으세요?

Do you have _____ questions?

② 나는 그들 모두 사랑합니다.

I love _____ of them.

③ 매일(모든 하루하루가)이 같아 보였다.

_____ day seemed the same.

④ 나는 그들을 둘 다 좋아하지 않는다.

I like _____ of them.

⑤ 그 소년들 중 누구도 지난 주말에 등산가지 않았다.

_____ of the boys went hiking last weekend.

A 다음 빈칸을 알맞은 영어 단어로 채우시오.

① I have two sons.

_____ is a doctor and _____ _____ is a nurse.

② There are three books on the table.

_____ is mine and _____ _____ are Mary's.

③ There are twenty students in the classroom.

_____ study English and _____ _____ study French.

B 빈칸에 알맞은 단어를 <보기>에서 골라 쓰시오.

<보기>	both	other	neither	one

① Kevin is from the States and Jason is from the States, too.

_____ of them are from the States.

② He doesn't like coffee and she doesn't like coffee, either.

_____ of them likes coffee.

C 다음 괄호 안에서 알맞은 것을 선택하시오.

① She's lost her umbrella. She has to buy (one / it).

② Would you have (some / any) tea?

③ I need (some / any) money but I don't have (some / any).

④ (Both / All / Every) dog has its day.

A. 다음 빈칸을 예시처럼 채우시오.

some / any		all	both
약간의 / 약간의, 어떤 ~도			
neither	none	every	each

B. 1번의 예시처럼 적절한 표현으로 빈칸을 채우시오.

① one   the other

② _____   _____

③ _____   _____   _____

C. 아래 문장들을 우리말로 해석하시오.

④ Both of them are from the States.

_____

⑤ One is mine and the others are Mary's.

_____

⑥ Would you have some tea?

_____

⑦ I need some money but I don't have any.

_____

정답 A의 정답은 앞 페이지의 오늘 공부했던 박스를 참고하세요. ② some, the others ③ one, others, the other ④ 그들 둘 다 미국 출신이다.
⑤ 하나는 내 것이다. 그리고 다른 것들은 Mary의 것이다. ⑥ 차 좀 드시겠어요? ⑦ 나는 돈이 좀 필요하지만 나는 돈을 하나도 가지고 있지 않다.

to부정사 1

1 'to + 동사원형'으로 문장 안에서 '~것, 하기, 할지'로 해석됨

    1) 주어 자리: (~것, ~하기, ~할지) + 은, 는, 이, 가

        예 To master English is not easy. = It is not easy to master English.

        To live in the city is fun. = It is fun to live in the city.

    2) 보어 자리: (~것, ~하기, ~할지) + 이다

        예 My hobby is to collect baseball cards.

        His dream is to be a baseball player.

    3) 목적어 자리: (~것, ~하기, ~할지) + ~을, 를

        예 She decided to visit her grandparents.

        He likes to eat some snacks at night.

    4) 의문사 + to부정사 : 의문사 의미 + 할지

        예 I don't know how to use it.　She knows when to start.

        I want to know what to eat.

혼공 팁

'의문사 + to부정사'는 '의문사 + 주어 + should(can) ~'으로 바꾸어 쓸 수 있다.

    예 I don't know how to use it. = I don't know how I can use it.

    She knows when to start. = She knows when she should start.

혼공 연습

 A <보기>와 같이 to부정사를 찾아 밑줄을 긋고 해석하시오.

> <보기> To live in the city is fun. ⇒ <u>To live</u> in the city is fun.
>
> 정답: 사는 것, 살기

① To master English is not easy.

정답: ＿＿＿＿＿＿＿＿＿＿＿＿＿＿＿＿

② My hobby is to collect baseball cards.

정답: ＿＿＿＿＿＿＿＿＿＿＿＿＿＿＿＿

③ His dream is to be a baseball player.

정답: ＿＿＿＿＿＿＿＿＿＿＿＿＿＿＿＿

④ She decided to visit her grandparents.

정답: ＿＿＿＿＿＿＿＿＿＿＿＿＿＿＿＿

⑤ He likes to eat some snacks at night.

정답: ＿＿＿＿＿＿＿＿＿＿＿＿＿＿＿＿

β 빈칸에 적절한 의문사를 쓰시오.

① I don't know ＿＿＿＿＿＿＿ to use it. (어떻게)

② She knows ＿＿＿＿＿＿＿ to start. (언제)

③ I want to know ＿＿＿＿＿＿＿ to eat. (무엇을)

A 우리말 의미와 같도록 주어진 영단어를 올바르게 배열하시오.

① 책 읽는 것은 때때로 지루하다.

(to / books / read / is / boring / sometimes)

_____

② Jun은 그 책을 사기를 원한다.

(wants / book / Jun / buy / the / to)

_____

B 다음 문장에서 어법상 <u>잘못된</u> 부분을 찾아 바르게 고치시오.

① It is good to working out every day.

_____

② I wanted to ate an apple pie.

_____

C 주어진 우리말과 같도록 영작하시오.

① 나는 너를 또 보길 희망한다.

I hope _____.

② 중국어를 배우는 것은 어려웠다.

It was hard _____.

③ John은 김치를 어떻게 먹을지 몰랐다.

John didn't know _____.

A. 다음 문장에서 to부정사를 찾아 밑줄을 긋고, 전체 문장을 우리말로 해석하시오.

① My hobby is to collect baseball cards.

_____

② It is fun to live in the city.

_____

③ His dream is to be a baseball player.

_____

④ She decided to visit her grandparents.

_____

⑤ He likes to eat some snacks at night.

_____

⑥ To read books is sometimes boring.

_____

⑦ I wanted to eat an apple pie.

_____

⑧ John didn't know how to eat kimchi.

_____

정답 ① to collect(내 취미는 야구 카드를 수집하는 것이다.) ② to live(도시에서 사는 것은 재미있다.) ③ to be(그의 꿈은 야구 선수가 되는 것이다.)
④ to visit(그녀는 그녀의 조부모님을 만나기로 결심했다.) ⑤ to eat(그는 밤에 간식을 먹는 것을 좋아한다.) ⑥ to read(책을 읽는 것은 때때로 지루하
다.) ⑦ to eat(나는 사과 파이를 하나 먹기 원했다.) ⑧ to eat(John은 김치를 어떻게 먹을지 몰랐다.)

to부정사 2

 혼공개념 to부정사의 형용사적 용법이란?

1 'to + 동사원형'으로 '~할, ~해야 할'로 해석됨

  1) 명사 뒤에서 수식

  예) I want <u>something</u> <u>to drink</u>.

   Please give me a <u>chance</u> <u>to study</u> English in Canada.

   I have a lot of <u>work</u> <u>to do</u> today.

  2) 뒤에 전치사가 같이 쓰이는 경우

  예) I need a friend <u>to talk with</u>.

   Can you give me something <u>to write with</u>?

   I'm looking for a bed <u>to sleep in</u>.

   Kevin bought a box <u>to put his things in</u>.

  혼공 팁

  위의 예문에서 마지막 전치사를 빼면 문법상 잘못된 표현이 된다. 'talk with a friend'와
  'talk a friend'를 비교하면 with(전치사)가 들어가는 것이 자연스럽다는 것을 알 수 있다.

  예) I need a friend <u>to talk</u>. (X)

   I need a friend <u>to talk with</u>. (O)

  3) It's time + to부정사 : ~할 시간이다

  예) It's time <u>to go</u> to sleep.   It's time <u>to go</u> to school.

   It's time <u>to have</u> lunch.

<보기>와 같이 to부정사를 찾아 밑줄을 긋고 해석하시오.

<보기>   I want something to drink. ⇒ I want something <u>to drink.</u>

정답: 마실

① Please give me a chance to study English in Canada.

정답: _____

② I have a lot of work to do today.

정답: _____

③ It's time to go to sleep.

정답: _____

④ It's time to go to school.

정답: _____

⑤ It's time to have lunch.

정답: _____

⑥ I need a friend to talk with.

정답: _____

⑦ Can you give me something to write with?

정답: _____

⑧ Kevin bought a box to put his things in.

정답: _____

A 빈칸에 내용상 적절한 단어를 쓰시오.

① I'm thirsty. I want something to _____.

② I'm hungry. I need something to _____.

③ I'm lonely. I need a friend to _____ _____.

β 우리말 의미와 같도록 주어진 표현을 올바르게 배열하시오.

① 몇 개의 앉을 의자들이 있다. (to / a few / there / sit on / chairs / are)

_____

② 나는 끝마쳐야 할 보고서가 둘 있다. (finish / to / two / have / I / reports)

_____

③ 이것은 내 가족들과 보기에 좋은 영화가 아니다.

(this / not / to / a good movie / my / watch / is / with / family)

_____

C 주어진 영단어를 활용하여 우리말 의미에 맞게 영작하시오.

① 나는 오늘 읽어야 할 책들이 많이 있다. (have, read)

_____

② 그녀는 앉을 쿠션이 필요했다. (need, sit)

_____

A. 다음 문장에서 to부정사를 찾아 밑줄을 긋고, 전체 문장을 우리말로 해석하시오.

① Please give me a chance to study English in Canada.

_____

② It's time to go to school.

_____

③ I have a lot of work to do today.

_____

④ I have two reports to finish.

_____

⑤ This is not a good movie to watch with my family.

_____

B. 다음 문장의 빈칸에 적절한 전치사를 쓰시오.

⑥ I need a friend to talk _____. (대화를 나눌 친구)

⑦ Can you give me something to write _____? (필기구)

⑧ Kevin bought a box to put his things _____.

⑨ There are a few chairs to sit _____.

정답 ① to study(저에게 캐나다에서 영어 공부를 할 기회를 주세요) ② to go(학교에 갈 시간이다) ③ to do(오늘은 내가 할 일이 많이 있다) ④ to finish(나는 끝마쳐야 할 보고서가 둘 있다) ⑤ to watch(이것은 내 가족들과 보기에 좋은 영화가 아니다) ⑥ with ⑦ with ⑧ in ⑨ on

to부정사 3

 혼공개념 to부정사의 부사적 용법이란?

1 'to + 동사원형'으로 가장 많은 의미로 쓰임

1) 목적: ~하기 위하여, 하기 위해(=in order to 동사원형)

例 I came here <u>to see</u> you.

Roy went to the library <u>to return</u> some books.

He practices Taekwondo every day (in order) <u>to stay</u> healthy.

혼공 팁

부사적 용법 중 '목적'은 같은 뜻을 가진 다른 문장으로 표현될 수 있다.

例 Roy went to the library (in order) <u>to return</u> some books.

= Roy went to the library <u>so that</u> he <u>could</u> return some books.

2) 감정의 원인: ~해서, ~하고서는

例 I'm <u>pleased</u> <u>to meet</u> you.

They were <u>surprised</u> <u>to hear</u> the news.

3) 형용사 수식: ~하기에

例 That hill was pretty <u>hard to climb</u>.

4) 결과: ~해서 (결국) ~ 하다

例 He grew up <u>to be</u> an architect.

(=and became)

혼공 연습

 <보기>와 같이 to부정사를 찾아 밑줄을 긋고 해석하시오.

<보기>   I came here to see you. ⇒ I came here <u>to see</u> you.

정답: 보기 위해서

① Roy went to the library to return some books.

정답: _____

② He practices Taekwondo every day to stay healthy.

정답: _____

③ She went to Italy to study architecture.

정답: _____

④ That hill was pretty hard to climb.

정답: _____

⑤ They were surprised to hear the news.

정답: _____

⑥ He grew up to be an architect.

정답: _____

다음 두 문장을 <보기>와 같이 한 문장으로 만드시오.

> <보기> Chloe went to Canada. She wanted to improve her English.
> ⇒ Chloe went to Canada to improve her English.

① He got up early. He wanted to go hiking.

_____

② She used my laptop. She wanted to do her homework.

_____

③ They left home early. They wanted to get to the airport on time.

_____

 다음 각 어구를 의미가 가장 자연스럽게 연결하시오.

① She was sad   ⓐ to catch the train.

② The movie was hard   ⓑ to break up with him.

③ She woke up early   ⓒ to understand.

 다음 주어진 단어를 활용하여 영작하시오.

① 그녀는 그녀의 자동차 열쇠를 찾아서 기뻤다. (glad, find)

_____

② 그 아이는 자라서 과학자가 되었다. (grow up, become)

_____

A. 다음 문장에서 to부정사를 찾아 밑줄을 긋고, 전체 문장을 우리말로 해석하시오.

① Chloe went to Canada to improve her English.

_____

② He practices Taekwondo every day to stay healthy.

_____

③ They were surprised to hear the news.

_____

④ She went to Italy to study architecture.

_____

⑤ Roy went to the library to return some books.

_____

⑥ That hill was pretty hard to climb.

_____

⑦ He grew up to be an architect.

_____

⑧ She woke up early to catch the train.

_____

정답 ① to improve(Chloe는 그녀의 영어를 향상시키기 위해 캐나다로 갔다.) ② to stay(그는 건강을 유지하기 위해 매일 태권도를 연습한다.)
③ to hear(그들은 그 소식을 듣고 놀랐다.) ④ to study(그녀는 건축학을 공부하기 위해 이탈리아로 갔다.) ⑤ to return(Roy는 몇 권의 책을 반납하기
위해 도서관에 갔다.) ⑥ to climb(그 언덕은 오르기 아주 어려웠다.) ⑦ to be(그는 자라서 건축가가 되었다.) ⑧ to catch(그녀는 그 기차를 잡기(타
기)위해 일찍 일어났다.)

too ~ to, enough to ~ 용법

💡 혼공개념 | too ~ to 용법이란?

1 too + 형용사 / 부사 + to + 동사원형 : 너무 ~해서 ~할 수 없다

(=so 형용사/부사 + that 주어 + cannot ~)

> 예 I am <u>too tired to walk</u>. ⇒ I am so tired that I cannot walk.
>
> The box is <u>too big to carry</u>. ⇒ The box is so big that I cannot carry it.
>
> The book was <u>too hard</u> for her <u>to understand</u>.
>
> ⇒ The book was so hard that she couldn't understand it.

혼공 팁

> so that용법으로 바꿀 때 that 이하의 문장이 의미상 완벽한지를 반드시 살펴봐야 한다.
>
> 예 I cannot <u>walk</u>.(O)　I cannot <u>carry</u>. (X)
>
> She couldn't <u>understand</u>. (X)

💡 혼공개념 | enough to ~ 용법이란?

1 형용사 + enough + <u>to + 동사원형</u> : ~할 만큼 충분히 ~한

(=so 형용사/부사 + that 주어 + can ~)

> 예 She is <u>old enough to go</u> there by herself.
>
> = She is so old that she can go there by herself.
>
> I was <u>lucky enough to pass</u> the test.
>
> = I was so lucky that I could pass the test.

A   <보기>와 같이 밑줄을 긋고 해석하시오.

<보기>	I am <u>too tired</u>	<u>to walk</u>.
	너무 지쳐서	걸을 수 없다

① The box is too big to carry.

_____   _____

② The book was too hard for her to understand.

_____   _____

B   <보기>와 같이 밑줄을 긋고 해석하시오.

<보기>	She is <u>old enough</u>	<u>to go</u> there by herself.
	충분히 나이든	갈 만큼

① The woman is strong enough to carry the box.

_____   _____

② I was lucky enough to pass the test.

_____   _____

C   다음 문장들을 우리말로 해석하시오.

① The book was so hard that she couldn't understand it.

_____

② I was so lucky that I could pass the test.

_____

A 다음 괄호 안에 too, enough 중 알맞은 것을 쓰고, 전체 문장을 우리말로 해석하시오.

① Mr. Kim was _____ sick to go to work.

_____

② It's warm _____ to go out for a walk.

_____

③ The food was _____ spicy for me to eat.

_____

B 다음 각 어구를 의미에 맞도록 연결하시오.

① He is fast enough   ⓐ to pick the apples.

② Ms. Kim is tall enough   ⓑ to watch the movie.

③ We are not old enough   ⓒ to run a mile in 5 minutes.

C 우리말 의미와 같도록 주어진 표현을 올바르게 배열하시오.

① 그녀는 너무 아파서 밖에 나갈 수가 없었다.

(sick / she / go out / was / too / to)

_____

② 그는 다른 사람들을 도와줄 만큼 충분히 친절하다.

(is / people / kind / he / to help / other / enough)

_____

A. 다음 문장을 우리말로 해석하시오.

① The book was so hard that she couldn't understand it.

_____

② I was so lucky that I could pass the test.

_____

③ It's warm enough to go out for a walk.

_____

④ The food was too spicy for me to eat.

_____

⑤ Ms. Kim is tall enough to pick the apples.

_____

⑥ The box is too big to carry.

_____

⑦ We are not old enough to watch the movie.

_____

⑧ He is kind enough to help other people.

_____

정답 ① 그 책은 너무 어려워서 그녀는 그것을 이해할 수 없었다. ② 나는 너무 운이 좋아서 그 결과 그 시험에 합격할 수 있었다. ③ 밖에 산책하러 나갈 수 있을 정도로 충분히 따뜻하다. ④ 그 음식은 너무 매워서 내가 먹을 수 없었다. ⑤ Ms. Kim은 그 사과들을 딸 수 있을 만큼 충분히 키가 크다. ⑥ 그 상자는 너무 커서 운반할 수가 없다. ⑦ 우리는 그 영화를 볼 만큼 충분히 나이 들지 않았다. ⑧ 그는 다른 사람들을 도울 만큼 충분히 친절하다.

동명사

 혼공개념 **동명사란?**

1 '동사 + ing'의 형태로 주로 '~하는 것', '~하기'의 의미로 쓰임

   1) 주어 자리: ~하는 것은

      예 <u>Playing</u> baseball is exciting.

   2) 보어 자리: ~하는 것이다

      예 My hobby is <u>collecting</u> stamps.

   3) 목적어 자리: ~하는 것을

      예 I like <u>reading</u> comic books.

   4) 전치사의 목적어: 전치사의 의미에 맞추어 해석

      예 I am sorry for <u>being</u> late.

혼공개념 **동명사만 목적어로 취하는 동사**

1 동명사만 목적어로 취하는 동사: enjoy, admit, practice,

                             mind, give up, finish, avoid, quit...

  예 He enjoys <u>playing</u> cards. (O)   He enjoys <u>to play</u> cards. (X)

혼공 팁

  동명사와 to부정사를 둘 다 목적어로 취하는 동사에는 시작(begin, start), 애정(like, love)
  등이 있다.

  예 It started <u>to snow(snowing)</u> in the evening.

혼공 연습

 A <보기>와 같이 밑줄 친 부분을 해석하시오.

<보기>	Playing baseball is exciting. 야구하는 것은

① My hobby is collecting stamps.

_____

② I like reading comic books.

_____

③ I am sorry for being late.

_____

④ He enjoys playing cards.

_____

B 다음 동사가 목적어로 취하는 것을 선택하시오.

① enjoy   + (to부정사, 동명사, 둘 다)

② begin   + (to부정사, 동명사, 둘 다)

③ avoid   + (to부정사, 동명사, 둘 다)

④ like   + (to부정사, 동명사, 둘 다)

⑤ finish   + (to부정사, 동명사, 둘 다)

⑥ give up + (to부정사, 동명사, 둘 다)

⑦ start   + (to부정사, 동명사, 둘 다)

⑧ want   + (to부정사, 동명사, 둘 다)

⑨ hope   + (to부정사, 동명사, 둘 다)

A 다음 문장에서 밑줄 친 단어를 어법상 알맞은 형태로 고치시오.

① I don't enjoy <u>drive</u> cars. _____

② Thank you for <u>help</u> me. _____

③ My parents were so proud of <u>teach</u> students. _____

β 괄호 안에 주어진 말을 동명사로 적절히 바꾸어 빈칸을 채우시오.

① I finished _____. (read the novel)

② _____ takes a long time. (learn English)

③ _____ is good for your health. (swim in the morning)

C 다음 괄호 안에서 어법상 알맞은 것을 고르시오.

① She avoided (answering / to answer) my questions.

② It suddenly began (raining / to rain) hard outside.

③ I'm sorry for (being / to be) stupid to you.

④ Mr. Kim didn't mind (waiting / to wait).

혼공
복습

A. 다음 문장들을 우리말로 해석하시오.

① I like reading comic books.

_____

② I am sorry for being late.

_____

③ Thank you for visiting me.

_____

④ I finished reading the novel.

_____

⑤ Swimming in the morning is good for your health.

_____

B. 다음 밑줄 친 부분을 어법상 올바른 표현으로 고치시오.

⑥ She avoided to answer my questions.

_____

⑦ I'm sorry for to be stupid to you.

_____

⑧ Mr. Kim didn't mind to wait.

_____

13

현재분사

1 '동사 + ing'의 형태로 쓰이며 진행형이나 명사를 수식하는 형용사로 사용함

   1) 진행형에 쓰일 때: ~하고 있는, ~하고 있는 중인

     [예] My uncle is <u>dancing</u> on the stage.

         They were <u>sitting</u> on the grass.

   2) 형용사로 쓰일 때: ~하는, ~하고 있는

     [예] The <u>singing</u> girl is my friend, Tina.

         The baby <u>sleeping</u> on the sofa is my brother.

   3) 목적보어로 쓰일 때

     [예] I saw my uncle <u>dancing</u> on the stage.

         I heard him <u>yelling</u> at them.

         My boss kept me <u>waiting</u> for a long time.

혼공 팁

동명사와 현재분사는 의미로 구분할 수 있다.

   [예] I like <u>reading</u> comic books.(동명사: ~하는 것)

       The <u>singing</u> girl is my friend, Tina.(현재분사: ~하는)

밑줄 친 부분을 우리말로 해석하시오.

① My uncle <u>is dancing</u> on the stage.

_____

② They <u>were sitting</u> on the grass.

_____

③ <u>The singing girl</u> is my friend, Tina.

_____

④ <u>The baby sleeping on the sofa</u> is my brother.

_____

⑤ <u>I saw my uncle dancing on the stage.</u>

_____

⑥ <u>I heard him yelling at them.</u>

_____

⑦ <u>My boss kept me waiting for a long time.</u>

_____

A 다음 문장에서 밑줄 친 단어를 어법상 알맞은 형태로 고치시오.

① The man (wear) sunglasses is my dad.

_____

② She had some (excite) news for me.

_____

③ There are a few people (wait) for the train.

_____

④ Mr. Anderson asked me an (embarrass) question.

_____

B 다음 빈칸에 알맞은 것을 <보기>에서 고르시오.

<보기>	walking	playing	chasing

① Look at the dog _____ the poor cat.

② I saw him _____ the piano all day long.

③ Can you see the boy _____ down the street?

C 우리말 의미와 같도록 주어진 표현을 올바르게 배열하시오.

① 나는 어떤 것이 내 팔에 닿는 것을 느꼈다.

(felt / I / my arm / something / touching)

_____

② 나는 그 아이들이 우는 것을 보았다. (saw / crying / I / the children)

_____

A. 다음 문장을 우리말로 해석하시오.

① My uncle is dancing on the stage.

_____

② The baby sleeping on the sofa is my brother.

_____

③ My boss kept me waiting for a long time.

_____

④ The man wearing sunglasses is my dad.

_____

⑤ Mr. Anderson asked me an embarrassing question.

_____

⑥ Look at the dog chasing the poor cat.

_____

⑦ Can you see the boy walking down the street?

_____

⑧ I felt something touching my arm.

_____

정답 ① 내 삼촌은 무대에서 춤추고 있다. ② 소파에서 자고 있는 그 아기는 내 남동생이다. ③ 내 상사는 나를 오랫동안 계속해서 기다리게 했다.
④ 선글라스를 착용하고 있는 그 남자는 내 아빠이다. ⑤ Anderson 씨는 내게 당황스러운 질문을 했다. ⑥ 그 불쌍한 고양이를 쫓고 있는 개를 봐라.
⑦ 당신은 거리를 걸어 내려가고 있는 저 소년을 볼 수 있나요? ⑧ 나는 어떤 것이 내 팔에 닿는 것을 느꼈다.

간접의문문

🔍 혼공개념 간접의문문이란?

1 의문문이 한 문장의 일부가 되는 것

    1) 의문사가 있는 경우: 의문사 + (주어) + 동사

        예 Can you tell me? + Where do you live?

          ⇒ Can you tell me <u>where you live</u>?

        Do you know? + When did he leave for Korea?

          ⇒ Do you know <u>when he left for Korea</u>?

        Tell me. + Who did it?

          ⇒ Tell me <u>who did it</u>.

> **혼공 팁**
>
> 의문사가 주어 역할을 하는 경우에는 '의문사 + 동사'로 간접의문문을 표현한다.
>
> 예 Tell me <u>who</u> did it. (누가)

    2) 의문사가 없는 경우: if / whether + 주어 + 동사

        예 I'm wondering + Is he in his room?

          ⇒ I'm wondering if(whether) he is in his room (or not).

    3) think, believe, guess, imagine, suppose와 같은 동사

        예 Do you think ~? + Where is Tom going?

          ⇒ Where do you think Tom is going?

혼공 연습

 다음 두 문장을 <보기>와 같이 하나의 문장으로 만드시오.

> <보기>　　　Can you tell me? + Where do you live?
>
> 　　　　　= Can you tell me <u>where you live</u>?

① Do you know? + When did he leave for Korea?

= Do you know _____?

② Tell me. ＋ Who did it?

= Tell me _____.

③ I'm wondering. + Is he in his room?

= I'm wondering _____.

④ Do you think? + Where is Tom going?

= Where _____?

⑤ I don't know. + Did Tom tell you about it?

= I don't know _____.

⑥ She couldn't remember. + Did she take her medicine?

= She couldn't remember _____.

A 우리말 의미와 같도록 주어진 표현을 올바르게 배열하시오.

① 그는 나에게 내가 그 선물이 마음에 드는지 물었다.

He asked me (I / the gift / liked / if)

_____

② Kevin은 내가 왜 그에게 화가 났냐고 물었다.

Kevin asked me (mad / him / I / at / was / why)

_____

③ 나는 그가 잘생겼는지 아닌지 모르겠다.

I don't know (or not / handsome / is / whether / he)

_____

B 다음 두 문장을 한 문장으로 만드시오.

① Do you know? + Which movie does she want to see?

_____

② He told me. + Who won the race?

_____

C 다음 문장을 우리말로 옮기시오.

① Who do you think the best teacher in your school is?

_____

② Please tell me what you are going to do this weekend.

_____

A. 다음 두 문장을 한 문장으로 만드시오.

① Do you know? + When did he leave for Korea?

_____

② I'm wondering. + Is he in his room?

_____

③ Do you think? + Where is Tom going?

_____

④ Tell me. + Who did it?

_____

⑤ Do you know? + Which movie does she want to see?

_____

⑥ He told me. + Who won the race?

_____

⑦ Kevin asked me. + Why was I mad at him?

_____

⑧ Do you think? + Who is the best teacher in your school?

_____

정답 ① Do you know when he left for Korea? ② I'm wondering if(whether) he is in his room(or not). ③ Where do you think Tom is going?
④. Tell me who did it. ⑤ Do you know which movie she wants to see? ⑥ He told me who won the race. ⑦ Kevin asked me why I was mad at him. ⑧ Who do you think the best teacher in your school is?

지각동사

 혼공개념 지각동사란?

1 생존을 위해 다른 대상이 어떤 행동을 하는 것을 감지하는 동사: see, hear, feel, watch, smell…

[예] I <u>saw</u> it. (지각동사 X)

I <u>saw</u> him dancing on the stage. (지각동사 O)

혼공개념 지각동사가 쓰이는 문장구조

지각동사 + 목적어(대상) + 동사원형 / 현재분사(~ing)

동사　　　　목적어　　　　　　목적보어

I　 smelled　　 something　　 burn(burning).
　지각동사　　　　목적어　　　 동사원형(현재분사)

[예] I felt a guy <u>come(coming)</u> toward me.

I watched him <u>enter(entering)</u> the room.

I heard her <u>cry(crying)</u>.

혼공 팁

목적보어에 동사원형이 오기도 하지만, 현재분사(~ing)가 올 때가 있다. 주로 끝나지 않은 동작(진행)을 강조할 때 쓰인다.

[예] We all felt the house <u>shaking</u>.

A 다음 괄호 안에서 어법상 적절한 것을 고르시오.

① I saw him (to dance / dancing) on the stage.

② I smelled something (burn / to burn).

③ I felt a guy (coming / to coming) toward me.

④ I watched him (enter / to entering) the room.

⑤ I heard her (cried / cry).

B 밑줄 친 단어를 알맞은 형태로 고치시오. (한 문제당 정답은 2개)

① I watched him <u>entered</u> the room.

_____, _____

② I saw them <u>studied</u> hard.

_____, _____

C 다음 단어들을 의미에 맞게 나열하시오.

① the / I / in / smelled / kitchen / something / burning

_____

② me / I / a / guy / felt / come / toward

_____

③ room / watched / enter / him / I / the

_____

A <보기>와 같이 두 문장을 한 문장으로 만드시오.

> <보기>   I heard him. He sang his favorite song.
>
> = I heard him sing his favorite song.

① I saw Kevin. He practiced Korean.

_____

② They felt the earthquake. It shook their house.

_____

③ I saw a puppy. It was crossing the street.

_____

 B 다음 문장에서 어법상 <u>어색한</u> 부분을 찾아 밑줄을 긋고 바르게 고치시오.

① I suddenly heard someone to call my name.

_____

② You can see him sang over there.

_____

C 다음 우리말에 알맞게 영작하시오.

① 나는 그들이 어떤 것을 적고 있는 것을 보았다.

_____

② 그녀는 John이 그녀의 이름을 부르는 것을 들었다.

_____

A. 다음 괄호 안에서 어법상 적절한 것을 고르시오.

① I saw him (to dance / dancing) on the stage.

② I smelled something (burn / to burn).

③ I felt a guy (coming / to coming) toward me.

④ I watched him (enter / to entering) the room.

⑤ I heard her (cried / cry).

B. 다음 문장을 우리말로 해석하시오.

⑥ I heard him sing his favorite song.

_____

⑦ They felt the earthquake shake their house.

_____

⑧ I saw a puppy crossing the street.

_____

⑨ I suddenly heard someone call my name.

_____

정답 ① dancing ② burn ③ coming ④ enter ⑤ cry ⑥ 나는 그가 가장 좋아하는 노래를 부르는 것을 들었다. ⑦ 그들은 지진이 그들의 집을 흔드는 것을 느꼈다. ⑧ 나는 한 강아지가 길을 건너는 것을 보았다. ⑨ 나는 갑자기 어떤 사람이 내 이름을 부르는 것을 들었다.

사역동사

💡 혼공개념 　사역동사란?

1 상대방이 어떤 동작을 하도록 하는 동사: let, have, make

[예] He <u>made</u> me happy. (사역동사 X)

He <u>made</u> me go home early. (사역동사 O)

💡 혼공개념 　사역동사가 쓰이는 문장구조

<u>사역동사</u> + <u>목적어(대상)</u> + <u>동사원형</u>
　동사　　　　　목적어　　　　목적보어

He 　had 　his kids 　wash their hands.
　사역동사　목적어　동사원형

[예] My parents don't let me <u>watch</u> TV at night.

The police officer made the man <u>get</u> out of his car.

💡 혼공개념 　준사역동사와 문장구조

<u>help(도움)</u> + 목적어 + <u>원형부정사</u> 또는 <u>to부정사</u>

<u>get(설득)</u> + 목적어 + <u>to부정사</u>

[예] He helped me <u>(to) do</u> my homework.

Our homeroom teacher got us <u>to get up</u> early in the morning.

I	make(강제) have(부탁) let(허락)	them	do	it.
	help(도움)		(to) do	
	get(설득)		to do	

혼공 연습

A 다음 표의 빈칸을 알맞은 사역동사로 채우시오.

_____(허락)	have(부탁)	_____(강제)

B 다음 문장에서 밑줄 친 부분을 어법에 맞게 고치시오.

① He had his kids <u>washing</u> their hands.

       _____

② He made me <u>gone</u> home early.

       _____

③ He helped me <u>doing</u> my homework.

       _____

④ Our homeroom teacher got us <u>to got up</u> early in the morning.

       _____

C 다음 표의 빈칸을 채우시오.

	make(_____)			
	have(부탁)		_____	
I	_____(허락)	them		it.
	_____(도움)		(to) do	
	_____(설득)		_____	

A 주어진 문장과 가장 관련이 있는 것을 ⓐ, ⓑ 중에서 고르시오.

① My uncle let me use his phone.

ⓐ 나는 전화를 걸 수 있었다.　　　ⓑ 나는 전화를 걸 수 없었다.

② Mr. Kim made me read the textbook aloud.

ⓐ 나는 교과서를 읽을 필요가 없었다.　　　ⓑ 나는 교과서를 읽어야 했다.

B 우리말 의미와 같도록 주어진 표현을 올바르게 배열하시오.

① 그 간호사는 내가 소매를 걷어 올리도록 했다.

(roll up / my sleeve / to / me / the nurse / got)

_____

② 그녀는 내가 그것에 대해 그만 말하도록 했다.

(it / stop / talking / she / about / me / had)

_____

C 주어진 표현을 참고하여 빈칸을 채우시오.

① His mom had him _____.

(folding the laundry)

② His mom made _____.

(cleaning his room)

③ His mom got _____.

(taking a shower)

A. 다음 표의 빈칸을 채우시오.

I	make(_____) _____(부탁) _____(허락)	them	_____	it.
	_____(도움)		_____	
	_____(설득)		_____	

B. 다음 문장들을 우리말로 해석하시오.

① My parents don't let me watch TV at night.

_____

② The police officer made the man get out of his car.

_____

③ Our homeroom teacher got us to get up early in the morning.

_____

④ My uncle let me use his phone.

_____

⑤ The nurse got me to roll up my sleeve.

_____

⑥ His mom had him fold the laundry.

_____

정답 A의 정답은 앞 페이지의 오늘 공부했던 박스를 참고하세요. ① 내 부모님들께서는 내가 밤에 TV 보는 것을 허락하지 않으신다. ② 그 경찰관
은 그 남자가 그의 차에서 나오도록 했다. ③ 우리 담임 선생님께서는 우리가 아침 일찍 일어나도록 했다. ④ 내 삼촌은 내가 그의 전화기를 쓰도록
허락했다. ⑤ 그 간호사는 내가 내 소매를 걷도록 했다. ⑥ 그의 엄마는 그가 빨래를 개도록 했다.

동사 + 목적어 + to부정사

💡 혼공개념　동사 + 목적어 + to부정사의 구조란?

1 want와 같은 종류의 동사를 써서 '~가 ~하기를 원하다'와 같은 의미로 사용함: want, ask, advise, allow, expect, forbid, order, tell...

| want
ask
advise
allow
expect
forbid
order
tell | 목적어 | to + 동사원형
(to부정사) | ~가 ~하기를 원하다
~에게 ~하라고 요구하다
~에게 ~하라고 충고하다
~에게 ~하는 것을 허락하다
~가 ~하기를 기대하다
~가 ~하는 것을 금지하다
~가 ~하라고 명령하다
~가 ~하라고 말하다 |

예 He wanted me to work out.　　She asked me to close the door.

He always tells us to study hard.　　Allow me to introduce myself.

My parents expect me to pass the test.

💡 혼공개념　부정하기

1 not + to부정사

예 My parents told me not to play computer games.

2 don't/doesn't/didn't + 본동사

예 She didn't ask me to close the door.

혼공 팁

to부정사를 부정할 때와, 본동사를 부정할 때의 의미가 다르므로 주의해야 한다.

혼공 연습

A 다음 표의 빈칸에 알맞은 동사를 쓰시오.

want _____ _____ _____ _____ _____ _____	목적어	to + 동사원형 (to부정사)	~가 ~하기를 원하다 ~에게 ~하라고 요구하다 ~에게 ~하라고 충고하다 ~에게 ~하는 것을 허락하다 ~가 ~하기를 기대하다 ~가 ~하는 것을 금지하다 ~가 ~하라고 명령하다 ~가 ~하라고 말하다

B 다음 단어들을 의미에 맞게 나열하시오.

① out / he / me / to / work / wanted

_____

② me / door / to / she / close / asked / the

_____

③ tells / to / always / study / hard / he / us

_____

C B에서 만든 세 문장의 to부정사를 not을 써서 부정하시오.

① _____

② _____

③ _____

A 다음 우리말과 같도록 빈칸에 알맞은 말을 쓰시오.

① 그 군인은 우리가 움직이지 않도록 명령했다.

The soldier _____ us _____ _____ _____.

② 내 아빠는 내가 거기에 혼자 가기를 원한다.

My dad _____ me _____ _____ there alone.

③ 그 의사는 내가 그 알약을 먹도록 충고했다.

The doctor _____ me _____ _____ the pill.

β 우리말 의미와 같도록 주어진 표현을 올바르게 배열하시오.

① 나의 부모님들께서는 내 여동생이 밤에 외출하는 것을 금하신다.

(to go out / forbid / at night / my sister / my parents)

_____

② Jason은 내가 그의 컴퓨터를 사용하도록 허락해주었다.

(to use / allowed / Jason / me / his computer)

_____

C 다음 괄호 안에서 어법상 알맞은 것을 고르시오.

① I want them (do / to do) their best tomorrow.

② She told me not (make / to make) the same mistake again.

③ The general ordered the soldiers (stay / to stay) silent.

④ Kelly asked me (subscribe / to subscribe) to her YouTube channel.

A. 다음 빈칸을 예시처럼 채우시오.

want ask advise allow expect forbid order tell	목적어	to + 동사원형 (to부정사)	~가 ~하기를 원하다 _____ _____ _____ _____ _____ _____ _____ _____

B. 다음 문장들을 우리말로 해석하시오.

① My parents expect me to pass the test.

_____

② He always tells us to study hard.

_____

③ My parents told me not to play computer games.

_____

④ She didn't ask me to close the door.

_____

⑤ Kelly asked me to subscribe to her YouTube channel.

_____

정답 A의 정답은 앞 페이지의 오늘 공부했던 박스를 참고하세요. ① 내 부모님께서는 내가 그 시험에 통과하기를 기대하신다. ② 그는 항상 우리가(우리에게) 열심히 공부하라고 말한다. ③ 내 부모님께서는 내가(나에게) 컴퓨터 게임을 하지 말라고 말씀하셨다. ④ 그녀는 내가(나에게) 문을 닫아 달라고 부탁하지 않았다. ⑤ Kelly는 내가 그녀의 유튜브 채널을 구독해달라고 부탁했다.

관계대명사 1

🔎 혼공개념 | 주격 관계대명사란?

① I know a boy. + ② He wants to be a doctor.

⇒ I know a boy _____ wants to be a doctor.
　　　　　　　선행사

⇒ I know a boy who wants to be a doctor.
　　　　　　　　주격 관계대명사

선행사의 종류	주격 관계대명사
사람	who(that)
사물	which(that)

예 Chloe is the teacher who(that) taught my daughter.

The room which(that) has a wonderful view is expensive.

The bus which(that) goes to Daegu has already left.

The girl who(that) is sitting next to the window is my girlfriend.

다음 두 문장을 <보기>처럼 관계대명사를 사용해서 한 문장으로 만드시오.

<보기>	I know a boy. + He wants to be a doctor. ⇒ I know a boy who(that) wants to be a doctor.

① This is my sister. She is a computer programmer.

_____

② The girl is Mary. She is sitting next to the window.

_____

③ The room is expensive. It has a wonderful view.

_____

④ The bus has already left. It goes to Daegu.

_____

⑤ Chloe is the teacher. She taught my daughter.

_____

⑥ The man is my dad. He is wearing sunglasses.

_____

A 다음 괄호 안에 주어진 말들을 올바른 순서로 배열하시오.

① The student _____ is Tom.

(cap / a / who / wearing / red / is)

② She is the lady _____.

(lives / door / that / next)

③ I have a daughter _____.

(likes / reading / who / novels)

B 다음 빈칸에 who, which, that 중 알맞은 것을 쓰시오. (답이 두 개인 경우도 있음)

① The guy _____ talked to me was very gentle.

② I want to go to a restaurant _____ opened recently.

③ You know what? Jason has a lot of shirts _____ are made in Vietnam.

C 다음 두 문장을 관계대명사를 사용해서 한 문장으로 만드시오.

① I know a store. It sells a lot of cheap items.

_____

② My grandfather runs a supermarket. It is one of the biggest in the town.

_____

③ The woman is my mom. She is looking at you.

_____

A. 다음 빈칸을 채우시오.

선행사의 종류	주격 관계대명사
사람	
사물	

B. 다음 빈칸에 적절한 관계대명사를 쓰시오.

① Chloe is the teacher _____ taught my daughter.

② The room _____ has a wonderful view is expensive.

③ The bus _____ goes to Daegu has already left.

④ The girl _____ is sitting next to the window is my girlfriend.

C. 다음 두 문장을 관계대명사를 사용해서 한 문장으로 만드시오.

⑤ This is my sister. She is a computer programmer.

_____

⑥ I know a store. It sells a lot of cheap items.

_____

정답 A의 정답은 앞 페이지의 오늘 공부했던 박스를 참고하세요. ① who(that) ② which(that) ③ which(that) ④ who(that) ⑤ This is my sister who(that) is a computer programmer. ⑥ I know a store which(that) sells a lot of cheap items.

관계대명사 2

혼공개념 | 목적격 관계대명사란?

① This is <u>the house</u>. + ② My dad built <u>it</u> last year.

⇒ This is <u>the house</u>. _____ My dad built last year.
　　　　　선행사

⇒ This is the house <u>which</u> my dad built last year.
　　　　　　　　목적격 관계대명사

선행사의 종류	목적격 관계대명사
사람	who / whom(that)
사물	which(that)

예 I'll give this watch to the boy <u>who(m)(that)</u> I like most.

Jake hopes to see the woman <u>who(m)(that)</u> he met in the park.

The watch <u>which(that)</u> my uncle gave to me is not working.

I returned the book <u>which(that)</u> I borrowed from the library.

다음 두 문장을 <보기>처럼 관계대명사를 사용해서 한 문장으로 만드시오.

<보기>   This is <u>the house</u>. + My dad built <u>it</u> last year.
    ⇒ This is the house <u>which(that)</u> my dad built last year.

① I'll give the gift to the boy. I like him most.

_____

② The watch is not working. My uncle gave it to me.

_____

③ Jake hopes to see the woman. He met her in the park.

_____

④ The book is on the table. She gave me the book.

_____

⑤ I am reading a novel. My father wrote it.

_____

⑥ I returned the book. I borrowed it from the library.

_____

A 다음 문장에서 목적격 관계대명사가 들어갈 곳에 V체크하고, 수식받는 명사에 밑줄을 치시오.

① The actress I like most is Julia Roberts.

② He found my wallet I lost on the street.

③ The house I lived in is near here.

β 다음 문장에서 관계대명사에 밑줄을 치고 생략 가능한지 체크하시오.

① Did she bring the umbrella that she left at her place?

(생략 가능 / 생략 불가능)

② The computer that Mr. Park bought three years ago is still working.

(생략 가능 / 생략 불가능)

③ The person who is sitting in front of you is Mr. Kim.

(생략 가능 / 생략 불가능)

C 다음 두 문장을 관계대명사를 사용해서 한 문장으로 만드시오.

① Kevin is the man. Chloe fell in love with him.

_____

② This is the email. My boss sent it to me.

_____

③ The man is handsome. She works with him.

_____

A. 다음 빈칸을 채우시오.

선행사의 종류	목적격 관계대명사
사람	
사물	

B. 다음 빈칸에 적절한 관계대명사를 쓰시오.

① I'll give the gift to the boy _____ I like most.

② He found my wallet _____ I lost on the street.

③ The person _____ is sitting in front of you is Mr. Kim.

④ Kevin is the man _____ Chloe fell in love with.

C. 다음 두 문장을 관계대명사를 사용해서 한 문장으로 만드시오.

⑤ Jake hopes to see the woman. He met her in the park.

_____

⑥ The man is handsome. She works with him.

_____

정답 A의 정답은 앞 페이지의 오늘 공부했던 박스를 참고하세요. ① who(m), that ② which(that) ③ who(that) ④ who(m), that ⑤ Jake hopes to see the woman who(whom, that) he met in the park. ⑥ The man who(whom, that) she works with is handsome.

관계대명사 3

💡 **혼공개념** | 소유격 관계사란?

① Look at the building. + ② Its windows are all red.

⇒ Look at the building _____ windows are all red.
　　　　　　　선행사

⇒ Look at the building whose windows are all red.
　　　　　　　　　　소유격 관계사

선행사의 종류	소유격 관계사
사람	whose
사물	whose / of which

예 She is the girl. + Her father is a pilot.

⇒ She is the girl whose father is a pilot.

An old woman lives next door. Her name is Mary.

⇒ An old woman whose name is Mary lives next door.

Look at the mountain. The top of it is covered with snow.

⇒ Look at the mountain of which the top is covered with snow.

A <보기>처럼 밑줄 친 부분과 관계있는 단어에 밑줄 치시오.

> <보기>   This is a car. + Its color is red.
>
> 정답: Its color is red.

① She is <u>the girl</u>. + Her father is a pilot.

② <u>An old woman</u> lives next door. Her name is Mary.

③ Look at <u>the mountain</u>. The top of it is covered with snow.

B A의 ①~③번 문장들을 소유격 관계사를 이용해서 한 문장으로 만드시오.

① She is the girl. Her father is a pilot.

_____

② An old woman lives next door. Her name is Mary.

_____

③ Look at the mountain. The top of it is covered with snow.

_____

A 다음 문장을 보고 같은 의미가 되도록 빈 칸을 채우시오.

① I have a friend _____ brother is a famous rapper.

I have a _____. _____ brother is a famous rapper.

② She met a boy _____ father ran a small store.

She met a _____. _____ father ran a small store.

③ John has a cat _____ hair is very long.

John has a _____. _____ hair is very long.

B 다음 우리말에 알맞게 주어진 표현들을 배열하시오.

① 나는 그녀의 사촌이 유명한 배우인 한 여자를 만났다.

(met / is / a woman / I / whose / a famous actor / cousin)

_____

② 그것의 지붕이 눈으로 덮인 그 집은 내 것이다.

(the house / covered with / whose / roof / snow / is / is / mine)

_____

C 다음 괄호 안에서 어법상 알맞은 단어를 하나 고르시오.

① The man (who / whose) is drinking coffee is my dad.

② I know a lady (who / whose) job is a teacher.

③ A man (who / whose) name is John will visit you.

A. 다음 빈칸을 채우시오.

선행사의 종류	소유격 관계사
사람	
사물	

B. 다음 문장들을 소유격 관계사를 이용해서 연결하시오.

① She is the girl. Her father is a pilot.

_____

② An old woman lives next door. Her name is Mary.

_____

③ Look at the mountain. The top of it is covered with snow.

_____

C. 다음 빈칸을 채우고 문장들을 우리말로 해석하시오.

④ She met a boy _____ father ran a small store.

_____

⑤ John has a cat _____ hair is very long.

_____

정답 A의 정답은 앞 페이지의 오늘 공부했던 박스를 참고하세요. ① She is the girl whose father is a pilot. ② An old woman whose name is Mary lives next door. ③ Look at the mountain of which the top is covered with snow. ④ whose(그녀는 작은 가게를 운영하는 아빠를 둔 한 소년을 만났다.) ⑤ whose(John은 털이 아주 긴 고양이를 가지고 있다.)

현재완료 1

1 과거에 한 행동이 현재에 영향을 미칠 때 사용함: have(has) + p.p.

　　1) ~를 막 했다, 끝냈다

　　* already, just, yet과 잘 쓰임

　　　　예 I have already finished my homework.

　　　　　　The restaurant has just opened.

　　2) ~해오고 있다

　　* since(~ 이후로), for + 시간/기간

　　　　예 She has played the piano for an hour.

　　　　　　I have learned English since I was 10 years old.

　　3) ~한 적이 있다

　　* been to + 장소, seen, ever, never, 횟수

　　　　예 Have you ever been to Japan?

　　　　　　I have seen a lion three times.

　　4) ~했고 (그 결과) 한 상태이다

　　* gone(가 버려서 여기 없다), lost(잃어버려서 없다)

　　　　예 I have lost my umbrella.

　　　　　　She has gone to the States.

Part 1

혼공 연습

A <보기>처럼 현재완료에 밑줄을 긋고 그 부분의 해석을 적으시오.

> <보기>　I have already finished my homework.
>
> ⇒ I <u>have</u> already <u>finished</u> my homework.
>
> 　　정답: ＿끝냈다＿

① I have lost my umbrella.

　　　　　　　　　　　　　　　＿＿＿＿＿＿＿＿＿＿

② She has gone to the States.

　　　　　　　　　　　　　　　＿＿＿＿＿＿＿＿＿＿

③ I have learned English since I was 10 years old.

　　　　　　　　　　　　　　　＿＿＿＿＿＿＿＿＿＿

④ I have seen a lion three times.

　　　　　　　　　　　　　　　＿＿＿＿＿＿＿＿＿＿

⑤ The restaurant has just opened.

　　　　　　　　　　　　　　　＿＿＿＿＿＿＿＿＿＿

⑥ Have you ever been to Japan?

　　　　　　　　　　　　　　　＿＿＿＿＿＿＿＿＿＿

⑦ She has played the piano for an hour.

　　　　　　　　　　　　　　　＿＿＿＿＿＿＿＿＿＿

다음 괄호 안에서 알맞은 것을 고르시오.

① Kevin (went / has gone) to Australia. I miss him so much.

② I (lived / have lived) in Seoul for seven years.

③ He (lost / has lost) his backpack 10 minutes ago.

 다음 우리말에 알맞게 주어진 단어들을 배열하시오.

① 어젯밤부터 비가 계속해서 내리고 있다.

(last / since / rained / it / has / night)

_____

② 그 남자가 내 지갑을 막 훔쳐갔어.

(man / stolen / the / has / my / just / wallet)

_____

다음 문장을 우리말로 해석하시오.

① I have known her for 10 years.

_____

② How many times have you been to China?

_____

③ I have never had a chance to visit your place.

_____

A. 아래 문장들을 우리말로 해석하시오.

① I have lost my umbrella.

_____

② I have known her for 10 years.

_____

③ I have learned English since I was 10 years old.

_____

④ I have never had a chance to visit your place.

_____

⑤ The restaurant has just opened.

_____

⑥ Have you ever been to Japan?

_____

⑦ She has played the piano for an hour.

_____

⑧ I have lived in Seoul for seven years.

_____

정답 ① 나는 내 우산을 잃어버렸다. ② 나는 그녀를 10년 동안 알아왔다. ③ 나는 10살 이후로 영어를 계속해서 배워왔다. ④ 나는 네 집을 방문할 기회를 절대 가져본 적이 없다. ⑤ 그 식당은 막 열었다. ⑥ 일본에 가본 적이 있니? ⑦ 그녀는 한 시간 동안 피아노를 계속해서 연주하고 있다. ⑧ 나는 서울에 7년 동안 살고 있다.

현재완료 2

 혼공개념 현재완료의 부정이란?

1 현재완료 표현에 not이나 never을 써서 부정하는 것: have(has) + not(never) + p.p.

[예] I haven't had breakfast yet.

My parents have never complained.

 혼공개념 현재완료의 의문문

1 (의문사) + have(has) + 주어 + p.p. ~ ?

[예] You have already finished the work.

⇒ Have you already finished the work?

대답: Yes, I have.(긍정) / No, I haven't.(부정)

혼공개념 현재완료의 부가의문문이란?

1 부가의문문: 말하는 사람이 자신의 의도를 표현하는 질문으로 문장 끝에 위치함

[예] You have never been to the States, have you?

He has done his homework, hasn't he?

2 대답하기: Yes(긍정), No(부정)을 활용

[예] You have never been to the States, have you?

대답: Yes, I have.(긍정) / No, I haven't.(부정)

He has done his homework, hasn't he?

대답: Yes, he has.(긍정) / No, he hasn't.(부정)

혼공 연습

A 다음 문장을 주어진 부정어를 써서 부정하시오.

① I have talked with him. (never)

_____

② My parents have complained. (never)

_____

③ I have had breakfast yet. (not)

_____

B 다음 문장을 의문문으로 만드시오.

① You have already finished the work.

_____

② Kevin has gone to Australia.

_____

③ The new hospital has just opened in our town.

_____

C 다음 문장의 빈칸에 부가의문문과 대답을 쓰시오.

① You have never been to the States, _____?

긍정의 대답: _____

② He has done his homework, _____?

부정의 대답: _____

A 다음 우리말과 같도록 빈칸에 알맞은 말을 쓰시오.

① 아빠는 벌써 저녁을 드셨어.

Dad has _____ _____ _____.

② Jason은 인사동에 네 번 다녀왔어.

Jason _____ _____ _____ Insadong four _____.

③ 나는 절대로 감기에 걸려 본 적이 없다.

I have _____ _____ a _____.

B 다음 사진을 보고 빈칸에 들어갈 알맞은 표현을 현재완료를 사용해서 쓰시오.

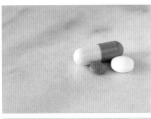

① A: Have you taken medicine?

B: No, _____.

② A: I haven't seen her lately.

B: You know what? She's

_____.

③ A: _____ _____

finished your _____?

B: No, I _____.

A. 다음 문장을 never 또는 not을 써서 부정하시오.

① I have talked with him. (never)

_____

② My parents have complained. (never)

_____

③ I have had breakfast yet. (not)

_____

B. 다음 문장을 의문문으로 만드시오.

④ You have already finished the work.

_____

⑤ Kevin has gone to Australia.

_____

⑥ The new hospital has just opened in our town.

_____

C. 아래 문장들을 우리말로 해석하시오.

⑦ Dad has already had dinner.

_____

⑧ Jason has been to Insadong four times.

_____

정답 ① I have never talked with him. ② My parents have never complained. ③ I have not(haven't) had breakfast yet. ④ Have you already finished the work? ⑤ Has Kevin gone to Australia? ⑥ Has the new hospital just opened in our town? ⑦ 아빠는 벌써 저녁을 드셨어. ⑧ Jason은 인사동에 네 번 다녀왔어.

비교급 1

 혼공개념 비교급이란?

1 비교급: 2개의 대상을 비교해서 차이가 있을 때 사용함

예 Kevin is t<u>aller</u> than Melanie.

 혼공개념 비교급 만드는 방법

1 대부분의 형용사, 부사: 원급(원래의 형태) + er

예 tall – tall<u>er</u>   fast – fast<u>er</u>   old – old<u>er</u>   kind – kind<u>er</u>

2 e로 끝나는 형용사, 부사: 원급 + r

예 large – larg<u>er</u>   close – clos<u>er</u>

3 자음 + y로 끝나는 형용사, 부사: y를 i로 고치고 + er

예 pretty – prett<u>ier</u>   dirty – dirt<u>ier</u>

4 '단모음 + 단자음'으로 끝나는 형용사, 부사: 마지막 자음 한 번 더 쓰고 + er

예 big – bigg<u>er</u>   hot – hott<u>er</u>   fat – fatt<u>er</u>

5 -less, -ish, -ful, -ous로 끝나는 2음절어 또는 3음절 이상의 긴 단어, '형용사 + ly' 형태

의 부사: more을 단어 앞에 씀

예 <u>more</u> famous   <u>more</u> colorful   <u>more</u> expensive

<u>more</u> beautiful   <u>more</u> slowly

6 불규칙 변화

예 good(well) – <u>better</u>   bad(ill) – <u>worse</u>   much(many) - <u>more</u>

다음 원급에 해당하는 비교급을 빈칸에 쓰시오.

	원급	비교급		원급	비교급
①	tall		⑮	fast	
②	old		⑯	kind	
③	large		⑰	close	
④	pretty		⑱	dirty	
⑤	big		⑲	hot	
⑥	fat		⑳	good	
⑦	bad		㉑	well	
⑧	ill		㉒	famous	
⑨	colorful		㉓	expensive	
⑩	beautiful		㉔	much(many)	
⑪	young		㉕	difficult	
⑫	heavy		㉖	important	
⑬	sad		㉗	loud	
⑭	smart		㉘	early	

Ⓐ 다음 원급에 해당하는 비교급과 우리말 해석을 쓰시오.

원급	비교급	해석
① young		
② difficult		
③ heavy		
④ important		
⑤ sad		
⑥ loud		
⑦ smart		
⑧ early		

Ⓑ 다음 <보기>처럼 문장을 완성하시오.

<보기>   Jack > Matthew (tall) ⇒ Jack is taller than Matthew.

① I > Kevin (strong)

_____

② my car > your car (expensive)

_____

③ Tom < Tom's brother (lazy)

_____

④ Jun > Jane (famous)

_____

A. 다음 빈칸을 예시처럼 채우시오.

	원급	비교급		원급	비교급
①	tall	taller	⑮	fast	
②	old		⑯	kind	
③	large		⑰	close	
④	pretty		⑱	dirty	
⑤	big		⑲	hot	
⑥	fat		⑳	good	
⑦	bad		㉑	well	
⑧	ill		㉒	famous	
⑨	colorful		㉓	expensive	
⑩	beautiful		㉔	much(many)	
⑪	young		㉕	difficult	
⑫	heavy		㉖	important	
⑬	sad		㉗	loud	
⑭	smart		㉘	early	

정답 A의 정답은 앞 페이지의 오늘 공부했던 박스를 참고하세요.

비교급 2

 혼공개념 비교급의 강조란?

1 비교급의 강조: 비교급 앞에서 '훨씬'이라는 의미로 비교급을 강조함

(much, a lot, even, still, far, by far...)

예 Jun is <u>much</u> stronger than Mike.

　　Jessica is <u>a lot</u> prettier than Cindy.

 혼공개념 원급 비교란?

1 원급 비교: 비교급과 달리 2개의 대상에 비슷한 점이 있을 때 표현하는 비교

예 Kevin is as <u>tall</u> as Jun.(Kevin과 Jun의 키는 비슷함)

1) as + 형용사/부사의 원급 + as

예 Jun has <u>as much</u> money <u>as</u> Dave.

　　Dogs run <u>as fast as</u> rabbits.

혼공 팁

원급 비교도 배수사(~배)를 사용하면 차이가 나는 비교를 할 수도 있다.

예 Jun has <u>three times as much</u> money <u>as</u> Dave.

2) as 원급 as + possible(as 원급 as 주어 + can): 가능한 한 ~하게

예 I drove <u>as slowly as possible</u>. = I drove <u>as slowly as I could</u>.

　　She eats <u>as much as possible</u>. = She eats <u>as much as she can</u>.

혼공 연습

 다음 문장에 much를 적절한 곳에 넣어서 비교급을 강조하시오.

① Jun is stronger than Mike.

_____

② Jessica is prettier than Cindy.

_____

③ Jack is taller than Matthew.

_____

β 다음 <보기>를 참고하여 영작하시오.

<보기>	Jun = Dave(much money)
	⇒ Jun has as much money as Dave.

① she = Kim Tae-hee(pretty)

_____

② dogs = rabbits(fast)

_____

③ Kevin = Jun(tall)

_____

④ Russia > Brazil(twice, big)

_____

A 다음 괄호 안에서 알맞은 단어를 선택하시오.

① I got home as (early / earlier) as possible.

② You have to study English much (hard / harder) than now.

③ The rabbit ran as (fast / faster) as he could.

B 우리말 의미와 같도록 주어진 표현을 올바르게 배열하시오.

① 이 건물은 저 건물만큼 높다.
(tall / this / building / that / one / is / as / as)

_____

② 그의 방은 내 것보다 훨씬 더 컸다.
(than / larger / his / much / mine / room / was)

_____

C 다음 사진과 주어진 단어를 보고 빈칸을 채우시오.

Jacob _____ Tyler.

(strong)

A. 다음 문장에 much를 적절한 곳에 넣어서 비교급을 강조하시오.

① Jun is stronger than Mike.

_____

② Jessica is prettier than Cindy.

_____

③ Jack is taller than Matthew.

_____

B. 아래 문장들을 우리말로 해석하시오.

④ Russia is twice as big as Brazil.

_____

⑤ I got home as early as possible.

_____

⑥ The rabbit ran as fast as he could.

_____

⑦ This building is as tall as that one.

_____

⑧ You have to study English much harder than now.

_____

정답 ① Jun is much stronger than Mike. ② Jessica is much prettier than Cindy. ③ Jack is much taller than Matthew. ④ 러시아는 브라질보다 두 배 더 크다. ⑤ 나는 가능한 일찍 집에 왔다. ⑥ 그 토끼는 그가 할 수 있는한 빨리 달렸다. ⑦ 이 건물은 저 건물만큼 높다. ⑧ 너는 지금보다 훨씬 더 열심히 영어를 공부해야 한다.

최상급

 **혼공개념** 최상급이란?

1 최상급: 3개 이상의 대상 속에서 가장 월등할 때 사용함

예 This is the <u>tallest</u> building in Korea.

혼공개념 최상급 만드는 방법

1 원급 + est, 원급(e로 끝나는 단어) + st

예 tall – tall<u>est</u>   fast – fast<u>est</u>   large – larg<u>est</u>   close – clos<u>est</u>

2 자음 + y로 끝나는 형용사, 부사: y를 i로 고치고 + est

예 pretty – prett<u>iest</u>   dirty – dirt<u>iest</u>

3 '단모음 + 단자음'으로 끝나는 형용사, 부사: 마지막 자음 한 번 더 쓰고 + est

예 big – bigg<u>est</u>   hot – hot<u>test</u>   fat – fat<u>test</u>

4 -less, -ish, -ful, -ous로 끝나는 2음절어 또는 3음절 이상의 긴 단어, '형용사 + ly' 형태
의 부사: most를 단어 앞에 씀

예 <u>most</u> famous   <u>most</u> colorful   <u>most</u> expensive

<u>most</u> beautiful   <u>most</u> slowly

5 불규칙 변화

예 good(well) – <u>best</u>   bad(ill) – <u>worst</u>   much(many) – <u>most</u>

혼공 팁

가장 뛰어난 여러 사람이나 사물 중 하나를 표현할 때, 'one of the 최상급 + 복수명사'라는
관용 표현을 쓴다.

예 Jun is <u>one of the most creative students</u> in our class.

다음 빈칸에 알맞은 단어를 쓰시오.

	원급	비교급	최상급
①	tall		
②	old		
③	large		
④	pretty		
⑤	big		
⑥	fat		
⑦	colorful		
⑧	beautiful		
⑨	young		
⑩	heavy		
⑪	sad		
⑫	smart		
⑬	fast		
⑭	kind		
⑮	close		
⑯	dirty		
⑰	hot		
⑱	famous		
⑲	expensive		
⑳	difficult		
㉑	important		
㉒	loud		
㉓	early		
㉔	good(well)		
㉕	bad(ill)		
㉖	much(many)		

A 주어진 단어를 참고하여 빈칸에 알맞은 단어를 쓰시오.

① This is the _____ building in our town. (old)

② Today is the _____ day of my life. (happy)

③ It was the _____ mistake he's ever made. (bad)

B 우리말 의미와 같도록 주어진 표현을 배열하시오.

① Seoul은 한국에서 가장 큰 도시이다.

(Korea / Seoul / is / the / city / biggest / in)

_____

② 그것은 그 해의 가장 더운 날이었다.

(year / it / was / of / hottest / the / day / the)

_____

③ 나일 강은 세계에서 가장 긴 강이다.

(is / the / the / longest / the Nile / river / in / world)

_____

C 다음 우리말과 같도록 빈칸을 채우시오.

① 그는 우리 반에서 가장 용감한 학생 중 한 명이다.

He is _____ of the _____ _____ in our class.

② BTS는 세계에서 가장 인기 있는 소년 밴드 중 하나이다.

BTS is _____ _____ the _____ popular boy bands in theworld.

A. 다음 빈칸을 예시처럼 채우시오.

원급	비교급	최상급
tall	taller	tallest
large		
pretty		
big		
heavy		
dirty		
colorful		
beautiful		
close		
hot		
famous		
expensive		
difficult		
important		
good(well)		
bad(ill)		
much(many)		

B. 아래 문장들을 우리말로 해석하시오.

① Today is the happiest day of my life.

_____

② It was the worst mistake he's ever made.

_____

③ The Nile is the longest river in the world.

_____

정답 A의 정답은 앞 페이지의 오늘 공부했던 박스를 참고하세요. ① 오늘은 내 삶에서 가장 행복한 날이다. ② 그것은 그가 지금껏 저질렀던 최악의 실수였다. ③ 나일 강은 세계에서 가장 긴 강이다.

had better / should

혼공개념 had better란?

1 had better + 동사원형: 주로 친한 사람에게 '~하는 게 낫겠다'라는 충고를 할 때 쓰는 표현

　예 You <u>had better</u> take this pill.

　　You <u>had better</u> go to the station now.

혼공개념 had better의 부정 및 축약

1 부정: had better + not + 동사원형

　예 You <u>had better not</u> smoke.

　　You <u>had better not</u> eat more *bulgogi*.

2 축약: had better를 'd better 형태로 줄여서 쓰기도 함

　예 It's too late. I'<u>d better</u> call my mom.

혼공개념 should란?

1 should + 동사원형: 이 행동이 좋은 것이고 바람직한 거니까 '~해야 한다'라는 의미를
가진 조동사

　예 We <u>should</u> listen to others.

　　I think you <u>should</u> watch this show.

　　Do you think I <u>should</u> buy some new clothes?

2 부정: should + not(=shouldn't)

　예 You <u>should not</u>(shouldn't) drink soda too often.

다음 문장에 had better, had better not을 넣어서 다시 쓰시오.

① You go to bed early. (had better)

_____

② You save some money. (had better)

_____

③ You eat more. (had better not)

_____

 축약형을 사용해 밑줄 친 부분을 다시 쓰시오.

① <u>You had better</u> drink enough water.

_____

② <u>You should not</u> be late for school.

_____

 다음 문장에서 should가 들어갈 위치에 V 표시하시오.

① You help people in need.

② You not drink soda too often.

③ You watch this show.

④ We listen to others.

you should + <보기>의 표현을 사용해서 빈칸을 채우시오.

<보기>	see	wear	work out	read

① _____ hard for your health.

② _____ a seat belt when you're driving.

③ _____ that book.

④ _____ the doctor.

B 우리말 의미와 같도록 주어진 표현을 배열하시오.

① 너는 다음 주유소에서 서지 않는 것이 낫겠다.

(not / the next / had better / stop / you / at / gas station)

_____

② 너는 네 신용 카드를 테이블 위에 두고 가서는 안 된다.

(on / shouldn't / you / your / the / credit card / table / leave)

_____

③ 우리는 균형 잡힌 식사를 해야 한다.

(we / diet / have / a / should / balanced)

_____

C 다음 사진을 보고 빈칸에 알맞은 표현을 써서 완성하시오.

Tom! The food is getting cold. I think

you _____ right now.

A. 아래 문장들을 우리말로 해석하시오.

① You had better go to the station now.

_____

② You had better not eat more *bulgogi*.

_____

③ It's too late. I'd better call my mom.

_____

④ Do you think I should buy some new clothes?

_____

⑤ You had better drink enough water.

_____

⑥ You should wear a seat belt when you're driving.

_____

⑦ You shouldn't leave your credit card on the table.

_____

⑧ You should work out hard for your health.

_____

정답 ① 너는 지금 역에 가는 것이 낫겠다. ② 너는 불고기를 더 먹지 않는 게 낫겠다. ③ 너무 늦었어. 나는 엄마한테 전화하는 게 낫겠어. ④ 너는 내가 새 옷을 좀 사야 한다고 생각하니? ⑤ 너는 충분한 물을 마시는 게 낫겠다. ⑥ 당신은 당신이 운전하는 동안 안전벨트를 착용해야 한다. ⑦ 너는 네 신용 카드를 테이블 위에 두고 가서는 안 된다. ⑧ 당신은 당신의 건강을 위해 열심히 운동해야 한다.

접속사 1

1 접속사: 단어, 구, 문장을 연결하는 역할을 하는 단어

before	~ 전에	after	~ 후에
(al)though	~에도 불구하고	if	만약에, ~인지
whether	~인지	unless	만약 ~ 아니라면

예 Don't forget to turn off the lights <u>before</u> you go out.

<u>After</u> he graduated, he got a nice job.

<u>Though</u> her parents didn't like her boyfriend, she loved him.

<u>If</u> you come to my house, I will show you my cats.

<u>If</u> it <u>rains</u> tomorrow, I can't go on a picnic.

<u>Unless</u> you are busy, help me with my homework.

= <u>If</u> you are <u>not</u> busy, help me with my homework.

혼공 팁

1. if가 '만약 ~한다면'이라는 뜻으로 쓰일 때에는 미래를 표현하더라도 will을 쓰지 않고 현 재동사를 쓴다.

예 <u>If</u> it <u>will rain</u>(X) tomorrow, I can't go on a picnic.

I don't know <u>if(whether)</u> he <u>will</u> come tomorrow.

2. if가 한 문장 속의 부분으로 '~인지'라는 의미로 쓰일 때 whether로 바꾸어 쓸 수 있다.

예 I don't know <u>if(whether)</u> he likes you or not.

A 다음 상자를 적절한 단어 또는 의미로 채우시오.

before	~ 전에		~ 후에
(al)though			만약에, ~인지
	~인지	unless	

B 빈칸에 주어진 의미에 맞는 단어를 쓰시오.

① Don't forget to turn off the lights _____ you go out. (전에)

② _____ he graduated, he luckily got a job. (후에)

③ _____ he is poor, he is always happy. (~에도 불구하고)

④ _____ it rains tomorrow, I can't go on a picnic. (만약에)

⑤ I don't know _____ he will come tomorrow. (~인지)

⑥ I don't know _____ he likes you or not. (~인지)

⑦ _____ you are busy, help me with my homework. (만약 ~ 아니라면)

C 다음 밑줄 친 부분을 어법에 맞게 고치시오.

① If it will rain tomorrow, I can't go on a picnic.

_____

② I don't know if he comes tomorrow.

_____

A <보기>에서 알맞은 말을 골라 빈칸에 쓰시오.

<보기>	you go to bed	it will be clear tomorrow
	she passes the test	you eat a meal

① Before _____, you should take a shower.

② I don't know if _____.

③ If _____, she will go to Paris.

④ You should brush your teeth right after _____.

B 다음 우리말과 같도록 빈칸을 채우시오.

① 당신이 그 컴퓨터를 사용한 다음에, 그것을 꺼주세요.

_____, please turn it off.

② 그것이 사실이 아니라면, 당신은 괜찮을 것이다.

Unless _____, you will be fine.

③ 그는 영어를 잘하는 데도 불구하고, 더 많은 언어를 배우고 싶어 한다.

_____, he wants to learn more languages.

④ 나는 이번 일요일에 비가 올지 모르겠다.

I don't know _____.

A. 다음 빈칸을 예시처럼 채우시오.

before	~전에	after	
(al)though		if	
whether		unless	

B. 아래 문장들을 우리말로 해석하시오.

① After he graduated, he got a nice job.

_____

② Don't forget to turn off the lights before you go out.

_____

③ If it rains tomorrow, I can't go on a picnic.

_____

④ I don't know whether he likes you or not.

_____

⑤ You should brush your teeth after you eat a meal.

_____

정답 A의 정답은 앞 페이지의 오늘 공부했던 박스를 참고하세요. ① 졸업한 후에, 그는 멋진 직장을 구했다. ② 나가기 전에 불 끄는 것을 잊지 마라. ③ 내일 비가 오면, 나는 소풍을 갈 수 없다. ④ 나는 그가 너를 좋아하는지 아닌지 모른다. ⑤ 너는 식사를 한 다음에 양치를 해야 한다.

접속사 2

💡 **혼공개념** | 접속사 2

when	~할 때	while	~하는 동안
because	~ 때문에	until	~ 때까지

예 When you get back, please give me a call.

While you were out, Jason cleaned your room.

I couldn't go to his birthday party because I was tired.

You should wait here until your dad comes.

We will stay inside until it gets dark.

혼공 팁

때나 조건을 나타내는 부사절에서는 미래 대신에 현재를 쓴다.

예 You should wait here until your dad comes.

We will stay inside until it gets dark.

💡 **혼공개념** | 접속사 that이란?

 한 문장의 부분으로서 단어가 아닌 또 다른 '한 문장'이 들어올 때 그 문장의 시작을 알리는 역할을 함

예 I think (that) Jun will come. (목적어)

That he likes his homeroom teacher is clear. (주어)

Jun is happy that she called him. (원인)

혼공 연습

A 빈칸에 의미에 맞는 접속사를 쓰시오.

① _____ you get back, please give me a call. (~할 때)

② _____ you were out, Jason cleaned your room. (~하는 동안)

③ I couldn't go to his birthday party _____ I was tired. (~ 때문에)

④ We will stay inside _____ it gets dark. (~ 때 까지)

B 다음 빈칸에 '원인' 또는 '결과'라고 쓰시오.

① I was late for school because I missed the bus.

   _____   _____

② My stomach got upset because I ate too much.

   _____   _____

③ Because I told him a lie, he is upset now.

   _____   _____

C 다음 문장에서 접속사 that이 들어갈 곳을 찾아 V표시 하시오.

① I think Jun will come.

② He likes his homeroom teacher is clear.

③ Jun is happy she called him.

A 빈칸에 가장 알맞은 단어를 <보기>에서 골라 쓰시오.

<보기>	when	because	until

① I am really tired _____ I stayed up all night.

② _____ you are free, please call me.

③ You must not drive a car _____ you turn 16.

B 접속사 that이 들어갈 곳을 찾아 V표시 하고, 우리말로 해석하시오.

① It is true the world is round.

_____

② All parents hope their kids are happy.

_____

③ He told me he did it on purpose.

_____

C <보기>에서 적절한 접속사를 골라 빈칸을 채우시오.

<보기>	while	because	until	that

My parents told me _____ Chloe called me several

times _____ I was out today. I couldn't call her back

_____ my phone suddenly stopped working. I waited

_____ my dad fixed it.

A. 다음 문장들을 우리말로 해석하시오.

① While you were out, Jason cleaned your room.

_____

② You should wait here until your dad comes.

_____

③ That he likes his homeroom teacher is clear.

_____

④ My stomach got upset because I ate too much.

_____

⑤ You must not drive a car until you turn 16.

_____

⑥ He told me that he did it on purpose.

_____

⑦ All parents hope that their kids are happy.

_____

정답 ① 네가 밖에 나간 동안, Jason이 너의 방을 청소했다. ② 너는 너의 아빠가 올 때까지 여기서 기다려야 한다. ③ 그가 그의 담임선생님을 좋아한다는 것은 분명하다. ④ 나는 너무 많이 먹어서 배탈이 났다. ⑤ 너는 16살이 될 때까지 차를 운전해서는 안 된다. ⑥ 그가 그것을 일부러 했다고 나에게 말했다. ⑦ 모든 부모님들은 그들의 아이들이 행복하기를 희망한다.

수동태 1

혼공개념 능동태, 수동태란?

1 능동태: 주어가 어떤 동작을 직접 하는 것

　[예] ① A dog bit Sara.

2 수동태: 주어가 어떤 동작을 당하거나, 영향을 입는 것

　[예] ② Sara was bitten by a dog.

혼공개념 수동태 문장 만들기

1 주어 + be + 과거분사(p.p.) + by 행위자

　[예] Amanda loves Shu.(능동 문장) → Shu is loved by Amanda.

2 목적어가 두 개인 문장: 두 개의 수동태 문장이 가능함

　[예] He gave me a ring.　　　　　　He gave me a ring.

　I was given a ring by him.　　　A ring was given (to) me by him.

혼공 연습

 다음 빈칸을 채우시오.

	원형	과거형	과거분사(p.p.)
①	love	loved	loved
②	bite	bit	
③	break	broke	
④	give	gave	
⑤	do	did	
⑥	choose	chose	
⑦	forget	forgot	
⑧	get	got	
⑨	find	found	
⑩	make	made	
⑪	send	sent	
⑫	see	saw	
⑬	wear	wore	
⑭	write	wrote	
⑮	eat	ate	
⑯	kill	killed	
⑰	use	used	
⑱	shake	shook	
⑲	steal	stole	

β 다음 문장을 수동태 문장으로 바꾸어 쓰시오.

① A dog bit Tom.

_____

② Amanda loves Shu.

_____

③ He gave me a ring.

_____

A 빈칸에 알맞은 말을 괄호 안에서 골라 쓰시오.

① _____ is used by _____. (a computer / Jason)

② _____ was written by _____. (my mom / the novel)

③ _____ was made in _____. (Italy / the table)

B 다음 문장을 수동태 문장으로 바꾸어 쓰시오.

① The earthquake shook the houses.

_____

② A tall guy stole my wallet.

_____

C 괄호 안의 표현을 활용하여 수동태 문장을 만드시오.

① 많은 동물들이 그 불로 인해 죽었다. (kill, the fire)

_____

② 곤충들은 때때로 우리에 의해서 먹혀진다. (insect, eat)

_____

③ 그 프로젝트는 그 팀에 의해서 행해졌다. (the project, do)

_____

A. 다음 빈칸을 예시처럼 채우시오.

원형	과거형	과거분사(p.p.)
love	loved	loved
bite		
break		
give		
do		
choose		
forget		
get		
find		
make		
send		
see		
wear		
write		
eat		
kill		
use		
shake		
steal		

B. 다음 문장들을 수동태 문장으로 바꾸시오.

① My mom wrote the novel.

_____

② The earthquake shook the houses.

_____

③ We sometimes eat insects.

_____

정답 A의 정답은 앞 페이지의 오늘 공부했던 박스를 참고하세요. ① The novel was written by my mom. ② The houses were shaken by the earthquake. ③ Insects are sometimes eaten by us.

수동태 2

💡 **혼공개념** 수동태 문장에서 행위자를 생략하는 경우

1 행위자의 생략: 행위자를 알 수 없거나, 일반인 행위자의 경우에는 'by 행위자'를 종종 생략함

[예] ① Someone killed him. (주어가 막연함)

② He was killed (by someone). (행위자 생략)

English is spoken all over the world (by us).

💡 **혼공개념** 수동태에서 by 이외의 전치사가 쓰이는 경우

표현	의미	표현	의미
be tired of	~에 싫증내다	be filled with	~로 가득 차 있다
be full of	~로 가득 차 있다	be covered with	~로 덮여 있다
be pleased with	~로 기뻐하다	be satisfied with	~로 만족하다
be interested in	~에 관심이 있다	be surprised at	~에 놀라다
be shocked at	~에 충격 받다	be worried about	~을 걱정하다
be known to	~에게 알려지다	be married to	~와 결혼하다

💡 **혼공개념** 조동사 + 수동태

1 수동태 앞에 조동사가 쓰여 의미가 더 풍부해짐

[예] The building can be burned.   He will be respected.

A 다음 문장을 행위자가 생략된 수동태 문장으로 바꾸어 쓰시오.

① We speak English all over the world.

_____

② Someone killed him.

_____

③ Something can burn the building.

_____

④ People will respect him.

_____

β 다음 빈칸에 우리말 의미를 쓰시오.

표현	의미	표현	의미
be tired of		be filled with	
be full of		be covered with	
be pleased with		be satisfied with	
be interested in		be surprised at	
be shocked at		be worried about	
be known to		be married to	

A 우리말 의미와 같도록 빈칸을 채우시오.

① 그녀는 Kevin의 책들에 관심이 있다

She _____ _____ _____ Kevin's books.

② 나는 나의 미래에 대해 걱정이다.

I _____ _____ _____ my future.

③ 내 부모님들께서는 그 결과에 만족할 것이다.

My parents _____ _____ _____ _____ the result.

④ 그 산의 꼭대기는 눈으로 덮여 있었다.

The top of the mountain _____ _____ _____ snow.

⑤ 그 건물은 부산에 지어질 것이다.

The building _____ _____ _____ in Busan.

B 다음 문장을 수동태 문장으로 바꾸어 쓰시오.

① You can buy clothes online.

Clothes _____.

② We called him Jun.

He _____.

③ The news surprised us.

We _____.

혼공
복습

A. 다음 빈칸을 예시처럼 채우시오.

표현	의미	표현	의미
be tired of	~에 싫증내다	be filled with	
	~로 가득 차 있다		~로 덮여 있다
	~로 기뻐하다		~로 만족하다
	~에 관심이 있다		~에 놀라다
	~에 충격 받다		~을 걱정하다
	~에게 알려지다		~와 결혼하다

B. 아래 문장들을 우리말로 해석하시오.

① He will be respected.

_____

② The building can be burned.

_____

③ English is spoken all over the world.

_____

④ She is interested in Kevin's books.

_____

⑤ Clothes can be bought online.

_____

⑥ He was called Jun.

_____

정답 A의 정답은 앞 페이지의 오늘 공부했던 박스를 참고하세요. ① 그는 존경 받을 것이다. ② 그 건물은 타버릴 수 있다. ③ 영어는 전 세계에서 사용되어 진다(구사되어 진다). ④ 그녀는 Kevin의 책들에 관심이 있다. ⑤ 옷(의류들)들은 온라인으로 구매될 수 있다. ⑥ 그는 Jun이라 불렸다.

혼공 기초 영문법
LEVEL 2
정답

1형식 문장

Part 1

A ① ~는 / ~한다 / 장소(우리는 / 산다 / 한국에) ② ~은 / ~한다 / 부사 (그 문은 / 열렸다 / 천천히) ③ ~는 / ~한다 / 시간(Linda는 / 조깅한 다 / 아침에) ④ ~가 / ~한다 / 장소 / 시간(나뭇잎 하나가 / 떨어졌다 / 땅바닥으로 / 아침에) ⑤ ~은 / ~한다 / 시간(그 꽃은 / 죽었다 / 어 젯밤에)

Part 2

A ① Jason / lives / in Russia(Jason은 / 산다 / 러시아에). ② The patient / died / suddenly(그 환자는 / 죽었다 / 갑자기). ③ They / work / on Saturdays(그들은 / 일한다 / 토요일에). ④ A lot of students / stood / in the playground(많은 학생들이 / 서 있었다 / 운동장에).

B ① The sun rises in the east. ② They go to school every day. ③ The taxi arrived at the hotel. ④ There were a lot of fans around him.

 2형식 문장

Part 1

A ① ~는 / ~되다 / 직업, 직책, 신분(그는 / 되었다 / 선생님) ② ~는 / ~ 이다 / 상태(너는 / 틀림없다 / 배고픈) ③ ~은 / ~되다 / 상태(잎들은 / 되었다 / 갈색) ④ ~는 / ~되다 / 상태(그 아기는 / 되었다 / 잠이 든) ⑤ ~는 / 감각동사 / 상태(그 스테이크는 / 냄새가 난다 / 좋은)

Part 2

A ① The soup / tastes / salty(그 수프는 / 맛이 난다 / 짠). ② My cousin / is / an English teacher(내 사촌은 / ~이다 / 영어 선생님). ③ The music / sounds / beautiful(그 음악은 / ~처럼 들린다 / 아 름다운). ④ Your dad / looks / really upset(너의 아빠는 / ~처럼 보인다 / 정말 화난).

B ① will, be, doctor ② taste ③ girl, looked, tired ④ was, hungry

 3형식 문장

Part 1

A ① ~는 / ~한다 / ~을(Harry는 / 청소했다 / 그의 집을) ② ~는 / ~한 다 / ~를 / 장소(나는 / 보았다 / 영화를 / 극장에서) ③ ~는 / ~한다 / ~를 / 장소(우리는 / 보았다 / 그를 / 공원에서) ④ ~한다 / ~를 / 장소 (두지 마라 / 모든 너의 달걀들을 / 한 바구니에) ⑤ ~은 / ~한다 / ~를 / 기타 / 시간(Jane은 / 팔았다 / 그 컴퓨터를 / 나에게 / 작년에)

Part 2

A ① Fine clothes / make / the man(멋진 옷이 / 만든다 / 사람을) ② My grandma / heated / the water / in the pot(내 할머니는 / 데웠 다 / 물을 / 냄비에 있는) ③ He / took / a bus / to Seoul / last night(그 는 / 탔다 / 버스를 / 서울로 가는 / 어젯밤에) ④ Kevin / blamed / me / for the mistake(Kevin은 / 비난했다 / 나를 / 그 실수로)

B ① reads, books, night ② put, salt ③ buy, bag, last ④ paid, this, watch

 4형식 문장

Part 1

A ① 그녀는 / 보냈다 / 나에게 / 편지를 ② 그는 / 사줬다 / 나에게 / 반지를 ③ Tom은 / 만들어줬다 / 나에게 / 장난감을 ④ Kevin은 / 물 었다 / 나에게 / 질문을 ⑤ 너는 / 사줄 수 있다 / 그녀에게 / 새 자동 차를 ⑥ 그녀는 / 보내야 한다 / 그에게 / 이메일을

Part 2

A ① My father / gives / me / a lot of advice(내 아버지는 / 주신다 / 나에게 / 많은 조언을). ② I / will tell / you / a funny story(나는 / 말해줄 것이다 / 너에게 / 재미있는 이야기를). ③ She / bought / me / a bicycle / for my birthday(그녀는 / 사주었다 / 나에게 / 자 전거를 / 내 생일을 위해(생일 선물로)). ④ My mom / made / him / an apple pie(내 엄마는 / 만들어 주었다 / 그에게 / 애플파이를).

B ① a kite for you ② English to me this year ③ tell the truth to us ④ She asked a lot of questions of me

 5형식 문장

Part 1

A ① ~는 / ~한다 / ~를 / 직업(내 엄마는 / 만들었다 / 나를 / 유명한 테 니스 선수로) ② ~는 / ~한다 / ~를 / 이름(내 할아버지는 / 이름 지었 다 / 나를 / Jun이라고) ③ ~은 / ~한다 / ~를 / 상태(그들은 / 페인트 칠했다 / 그 벽들을 / 파란색으로) ④ ~는 / ~한다 / ~를 / 상태(이 재 킷은 / 유지시켜 줄 것이다 / 당신을 / 따뜻한 ⑤ ~는 / ~한다 / ~가 / 동작(박 선생님은 / 도왔다 / 우리가 / 그 차를 세차하도록) ⑥ ~는 / ~한다 / ~가 / 동작(그녀는 / 만들었다 / Chloe가 / 그 책을 읽도록)

Part 2

A ① Jun / always makes / us / laugh(Jun은 / 항상 만든다 / 우리를 / 웃도록). ② Jogging / can keep / you / healthy(조깅은 / 유지시 킬 수 있다 / 너를 / 건강한). ③ We / called / him / Jack(우리는 / 불렀다 / 그를 / Jack이라고). ④ My parents / didn't allow / me / to go out(내 부모님들은 / 허락하지 않았다 / 내가 / 나가도록).

B ① paint my house white ② helped me (to) solve ③ keep your body strong ④ We elected Cindy

 재귀대명사

Part 1

A ① myself, herself ② himself, itself ③ yourself, yourselves ④ ourselves, themselves

B ① myself ② herself ③ himself ④ ourselves

C ① 그녀는 그것을 혼자 했다. ② 우리는 파티에서 즐거운 시간을 보냈다. ③ 너는 행동을 바르게 해야 한다.

Part 2

A ① myself, X ② herself, X ③ itself, O ④ themselves, X ⑤ himself, O

B ① help, yourself ② herself, door ③ old, cook, herself

 07 부정대명사

Part 1

A ① all, both ② some, every ③ each, both ④ neither, every ⑤ any, none

B ① any ② all ③ Every ④ neither ⑤ None

Part 2

A ① One, the, other ② One, the, others ③ Some, the, others

B ① Both ② Neither

C ① one ② some ③ some, any ④ Every

 08 to부정사 1

Part 1

A ① To master, 통달하는 것(통달하기) ② to collect, 수집하는 것(수집하기) ③ to be, 되는 것(되기) ④ to visit, 방문하는 것(방문하기) ⑤ to eat, 먹는 것(먹기)

B ① how ② when ③ what

Part 2

A ① To read books is sometimes boring. ② Jun wants to buy the book.

B ① working → work ② ate → eat

C ① to see you again ② to learn Chinese ③ how to eat kimchi

 09 to부정사 2

Part 1

A ① to study, 공부할 ② to do, 할 ③ to go, 갈 ④ to go, 갈 ⑤ to have, 먹을(가질, 할) ⑥ to talk with, 함께 이야기 나눌 ⑦ to write with, 쓸(필기구) ⑧ to put, 둘(넣을)

Part 2

A ① drink ② eat ③ talk, with

B ① There are a few chairs to sit on. ② I have two reports to finish. ③ This is not a good movie to watch with my family.

C ① I have many(a lot of) books to read today. ② She needed a cushion to sit on.

 10 to부정사 3

Part 1

A ① to return, 반납하기 위해 ② to stay, 유지하기 위해 ③ to study, 공부하기 위해 ④ to climb, 오르기 ⑤ to hear, 듣고서는 ⑥ to be, (그 결과) 되었다

Part 2

A ① He got up early to go hiking. ② She used my laptop to do her homework. ③ They left home early to get to the airport on time.

B ① b ② c ③ a

C ① She was glad to find her car key. ② The child grew up to become a scientist.

 11 too ~ to, enough to 용법

Part 1

A ① too big, to carry(너무 커서, 운반할 수 없다) ② too hard, to understand(너무 어려워서, 이해할 수 없다)

B ① strong enough, to carry(충분히 강한, 운반할 만큼) ② lucky enough, to pass(충분히 운이 좋은, 통과할 만큼)

C ① 그 책은 너무 어려워서 그녀는 그것을 이해할 수 없었다. ② 나는 너무 운이 좋아서 그 결과 그 시험에 합격할 수 있었다.

Part 2

A ① too, Mr. Kim은 너무 아파서 출근할 수 없었다. ② enough, 밖에 산책하러 나갈 수 있을 정도로 충분히 따뜻하다. ③ too, 그 음식은 너무 매워서 내가 먹을 수 없었다.

B ① c ② a ③ b

C ① She was too sick to go out. ② He is kind enough to help other people.

 12 동명사

Part 1

A ① 우표 수집하는 것이다 ② 만화책을 읽는 것을 ③ 늦어서 ④ 카드 놀이를

B ① 동명사 ② 둘 다 ③ 동명사 ④ 둘 다 ⑤ 동명사 ⑥ 동명사 ⑦ 둘 다 ⑧ to부정사 ⑨ to부정사

Part 2

A ① driving ② helping ③ teaching

B ① reading the novel ② Learning English ③ Swimming in the morning

C ① answering ② raining, to rain ③ being ④ waiting

13 현재분사

Part 1

A ① 춤추고 있는 중이다 ② 앉아 있는 중이었다 ③ 그 노래 부르는 소녀는 ④ 소파에서 자고 있는 그 아기는 ⑤ 나는 내 삼촌이 무대에서 춤추고 있는 것을 보았다. ⑥ 나는 그가 그들에게 고함치는 것을 들었다. ⑦ 내 상사는 나를 오랫동안 계속해서 기다리게 했다.

Part 2

A ① wearing ② exciting ③ waiting ④ embarrassing

B ① chasing ② playing ③ walking

C ① I felt something touching my arm. ② I saw the children crying.

14 간접의문문

Part 1

A ① when he left for Korea ② who did it ③ if(whether) he is in his room(or not) ④ do you think Tom is going ⑤ if(whether) Tom told you about it(or not) ⑥ if(whether) she took her medicine(or not)

Part 2

A ① if I liked the gift ② why I was mad at him ③ whether he is handsome or not

B ① Do you know which movie she wants to see? ② He told me who won the race.

C ① 너는 누가 너의 학교에서 가장 좋은 선생님이라 생각하니? ② 네가 이번 주말에 무엇을 할지 나에게 말해줘.

15 지각동사

Part 1

A ① dancing ② burn ③ coming ④ enter ⑤ cry

B ① enter, entering ② study, studying

C ① I smelled something burning in the kitchen. ② I felt a guy come toward me. ③ I watched him enter the room.

Part 2

A ① I saw Kevin practice Korean. ② They felt the earthquake shake their house. ③ I saw a puppy crossing the street.

B ① to call → call(calling) ② sang → sing(singing)

C ① I saw them write(writing) something. ② She heard John call(calling) her name.

16 사역동사

Part 1

A let, make

B ① wash ② go ③ (to) do ④ to get up

C 앞 페이지의 박스를 참고하세요.

Part 2

A ① a ② b

B ① The nurse got me to roll up my sleeve. ② She had me stop talking about it.

C ① fold the laundry ② him clean his room ③ him to take a shower

17 동사+목적어+to부정사

Part 1

A 본문 75쪽 표를 참고하세요.

B ① He wanted me to work out. ② She asked me to close the door. ③ He always tells us to study hard.

C ① He wanted me not to work out. ② She asked me not to close the door. ③ He always tells us not to study hard.

Part 2

A ① ordered, not, to, move ② wants, to, go ③ advised, to, take

B ① My parents forbid my sister to go out at night. ② Jason allowed me to use his computer.

C ① to do ② to make ③ to stay ④ to subscribe

18 관계대명사 1

Part 1

A ① This is my sister who(that) is a computer programmer. ② The girl who(that) is sitting next to the window is Mary. ③ The room which(that) has a wonderful view is expensive. ④ The bus which(that) goes to Daegu has already left. ⑤ Chloe is the teacher who(that) taught my daughter. ⑥ The man who(that) is wearing sunglasses is my dad.

Part 2

A ① who is wearing a red cap ② that lives next door ③ who likes reading novels

B ① who(that) ② which(that) ③ which(that)

C ① I know a store which(that) sells a lot of cheap items. ② My grandfather runs a supermarket which(that) is one of the biggest in the town. ③ The woman who(that) is looking at you is my mom.

C ① 나는 그녀를 10년째 알고 있다(지내고 있다). ② 너는 중국에 몇 번 가본 적이 있니? ③ 나는 네 집을 방문할 기회를 절대 가져본 적이 없다.

 19 관계대명사 2

Part 1

A ① I'll give the gift to the boy who(whom, that) I like most. ② The watch which(that) my uncle gave to me is not working. ③ Jake hopes to see the woman who(whom, that) he met in the park. ④ The book which(that) she gave me is on the table. ⑤ I am reading a novel which(that) my father wrote. ⑥ I returned the book which(that) I borrowed from the library.

Part 2

A ① The actress ∨ I like most is Julia Roberts. ② He found my wallet ∨ I lost on the street. ③ The house ∨ I lived in is near here.

B ① that, 생략 가능 ② that, 생략 가능 ③ who, 생략 불가능

C ① Kevin is the man who(whom, that) Chloe fell in love with. ② This is the email which(that) my boss sent to me. ③ The man who(whom, that) she works with is handsome.

 20 관계대명사 3

Part 1

A ① Her father is a pilot. ② Her name is Mary. ③ The top of it is covered with snow.

B ① She is the girl whose father is a pilot. ② An old woman whose name is Mary lives next door. ③ Look at the mountain of which the top is covered with snow.

Part 2

A ① whose, friend, His(Her) ② whose, boy, His ③ whose, cat, Its

B ① I met a woman whose cousin is a famous actor. ② The house whose roof is covered with snow is mine.

C ① who ② whose ③ whose

 21 현재완료 1

Part 1

A ① I have lost my umbrella. 잃어버렸다. ② She has gone to the States. 가 버렸다. ③ I have learned English since I was 10 years old. 배워왔다. ④ I have seen a lion three times. 본 적이 있다. ⑤ The restaurant has just opened. 열었다. ⑥ Have you ever been to Japan? 가본 적이 있니? ⑦ She has played the piano for an hour. 연주하고 있다.

Part 2

A ① has gone ② have lived ③ lost

B ① It has rained since last night. ② The man has just stolen my wallet.

 22 현재완료 2

Part 1

A ① I have never talked with him. ② My parents have never complained. ③ I have not(haven't) had breakfast yet.

B ① Have you already finished the work? ② Has Kevin gone to Australia? ③ Has the new hospital just opened in our town?

C ① have you / Yes, I have. ② hasn't he / No, he hasn't.

Part 2

A ① already, had, dinner ② has, been, to, times ③ never, caught, cold

B ① I haven't(have not) ② gone to Paris ③ Have, you, homework, haven't

 23 비교급 1

Part 1

A ① taller ② older ③ larger ④ prettier ⑤ bigger ⑥ fatter ⑦ worse ⑧ worse ⑨ more colorful ⑩ more beautiful ⑪ younger ⑫ heavier ⑬ sadder ⑭ smarter ⑮ faster ⑯ kinder ⑰ closer ⑱ dirtier ⑲ hotter ⑳ better ㉑ better ㉒ more famous ㉓ more expensive ㉔ more ㉕ more difficult ㉖ more important ㉗ louder ㉘ earlier

Part 2

A ① younger, 더 젊은(어린) ② more difficult, 더 어려운 ③ heavier, 더 무거운 ④ more important, 더 중요한 ⑤ sadder, 더 슬픈 ⑥ louder, 더 시끄러운(큰) ⑦ smarter, 더 똑똑한 ⑧ earlier, 더 이른(일찍)

B ① I am stronger than Kevin. ② My car is more expensive than your car. ③ Tom's brother is lazier than Tom. ④ Jun is more famous than Jane.

24 비교급 2

Part 1

A ① Jun is much stronger than Mike. ② Jessica is much prettier than Cindy. ③ Jack is much taller than Matthew.

B ① She is as pretty as Kim Tae-hee. ② Dogs run as fast as rabbits. ③ Kevin is as tall as Jun. ④ Russia is twice as big as Brazil.

Part 2

A ① early ② harder ③ fast

B ① This building is as tall as that one. ② His room was much larger than mine.

C is as strong as

최상급

Part 1

A ① 교재 23강 또는 인터넷 강의를 참고하세요.

Part 2

A ① oldest ② happiest ③ worst

B ① Seoul is the biggest city in Korea. ② It was the hottest day of the year. ③ The Nile is the longest river in the world.

C ① one, bravest, students ② one, of, most

 had better / should

Part 1

A ① You had better go to bed early. ② You had better save some money. ③ You had better not eat more.

B ① You'd better ② You shouldn't

C ① You ✓ help people in need. ② You ✓ not drink soda too often. ③ You ✓ watch this show. ④ We ✓ listen to others.

Part 2

A ① You should work out ② You should wear ③ You should read ④ You should see

B ① You had better not stop at the next gas station.
② You shouldn't leave your credit card on the table.
③ We should have a balanced diet.

C should eat

 접속사 1

Part 1

A 본문 115쪽 표를 참고하세요.

B ① before ② After ③ Though(Although) ④ If ⑤ whether (if) ⑥ whether(if) ⑦ Unless

C ① rains ② will come

Part 2

A ① you go to bed ② it will be clear tomorrow ③ she passes the test ④ you eat a meal

B ① After you use the computer ② it is true ③ Though (Although) he is good at English ④ whether(if) it will rain this Sunday

 접속사 2

Part 1

A ① When ② While ③ because ④ until

B ① 결과, 원인 ② 결과, 원인 ③ 원인, 결과

C ① I think ✓ Jun will come. ② He likes ✓ his homeroom teacher is clear. 또는 He likes ✓ his homeroom teacher is clear. ③ Jun is happy ✓ she called him.

Part 2

A ① because ② When ③ until

B ① It is true ✓ the world is round. 지구가 둥글다는 것은 사실이다.
② All parents hope ✓ their kids are happy. 모든 부모님들은 그들의 아이들이 행복하기를 희망한다. ③ He told me ✓ he did it on purpose. 그가 그것을 일부러 했다고 나에게 말했다.

C that, while, because, until

 수동태 1

Part 1

A ② bitten ③ broken ④ given ⑤ done ⑥ chosen ⑦ forgotten ⑧ got(gotten) ⑨ found ⑩ made ⑪ sent ⑫ seen ⑬ worn ⑭ written ⑮ eaten ⑯ killed ⑰ used ⑱ shaken ⑲ stolen

B ① Tom was bitten by a dog. ② Shu is loved by Amanda. ③ I was given a ring by him. A ring was given (to) me by him.

Part 2

A ① A computer, Jason ② The novel, my mom ③ The table, Italy

B ① The houses were shaken by the earthquake. ② My wallet was stolen by a tall guy.

C ① Many(A lot of) animals were killed by the fire.
② Insects are sometimes eaten by us.
③ The project was done by the team.

(30) 수동태 2

Part 1

A ① English is spoken all over the world (by us). ② He was killed (by someone). ③ The building can be burned (by something). ④ He will be respected (by people).

B 본문 127쪽 표를 참고하세요.

Part 2

A ① is, interested, in ② am, worried, about ③ will, be, satisfied, with ④ was, covered, with ⑤ will, be, built

B ① can be bought online (by you) ② was called Jun (by us)
③ were surprised at the news